PASSBOOK® SERIES

C000020471

THE *PASSBOOK® SERIES* has been created to prepare applicants and candidates for the ultimate academic battlefield – the examination room.

At some time in our lives, each and every one of us may be required to take an examination – for validation, matriculation, admission, qualification, registration, certification, or licensure.

Based on the assumption that every applicant or candidate has met the basic formal educational standards, has taken the required number of courses, and read the necessary texts, the *PASSBOOK® SERIES* furnishes the one special preparation which may assure passing with confidence, instead of failing with insecurity. Examination questions – together with answers – are furnished as the basic vehicle for study so that the mysteries of the examination and its compounding difficulties may be eliminated or diminished by a sure method.

This book is meant to help you pass your examination provided that you qualify and are serious in your objective.

The entire field is reviewed through the huge store of content information which is succinctly presented through a provocative and challenging approach – the question-and-answer method.

A climate of success is established by furnishing the correct answers at the end of each test.

You soon learn to recognize types of questions, forms of questions, and patterns of questioning. You may even begin to anticipate expected outcomes.

You perceive that many questions are repeated or adapted so that you can gain acute insights, which may enable you to score many sure points.

You learn how to confront new questions, or types of questions, and to attack them confidently and work out the correct answers.

You note objectives and emphases, and recognize pitfalls and dangers, so that you may make positive educational adjustments.

Moreover, you are kept fully informed in relation to new concepts, methods, practices, and directions in the field.

You discover that you arre actually taking the examination all the time: you are preparing for the examination by "taking" an examination, not by reading extraneous and/or supererogatory textbooks.

In short, this PASSBOOK®, used directedly, should be an important factor in helping you to pass your test.

CAREER EXAMINATION SERIES

THIS IS YOUR **PASSBOOK**® FOR ...

LEGAL ASSISTANT I

NLC®

NATIONAL LEARNING CORPORATION®
passbooks.com

LEGAL ASSISTANT I

Duties

As a Legal Assistant I, under the direction of staff attorneys in various areas of law, you would be responsible for compiling and organizing documentation; preparing and assisting in the preparation of legal documents and forms; ensuring court documents, including judgments, are properly and timely filed; logging information; and preparing correspondence and subpoenas. You would respond to inquiries and complaints, track cases, ensure that deadlines are met, and maintain various calendars. You would conduct research into legal matters, analyze materials, and present both verbal and written comments on your findings. You might prepare and maintain files, interview witnesses and clients, record and monitor the status of legislation, and gather and create materials and summaries of legislation and current legal developments pertinent to the agency. The use of computer software and the Internet is integral to these positions and may be used in any of the following areas: preparing documents, creating or updating databases or spreadsheets, tracking and researching assignments or litigation, and communicating. This position requires the ability to work independently on some matters/assignments.

SUBJECT OF EXAMINATION
The written test is designed to test for knowledge, skills, and/or abilities in such areas as:
1. Conducting research into legal matters;
2. Legal terminology, documents and forms;
3. Preparing written material;
4. Office record keeping; and
5. Interviewing.

HOW TO TAKE A TEST

I. YOU MUST PASS AN EXAMINATION

A. *WHAT EVERY CANDIDATE SHOULD KNOW*

Examination applicants often ask us for help in preparing for the written test. What can I study in advance? What kinds of questions will be asked? How will the test be given? How will the papers be graded?

As an applicant for a civil service examination, you may be wondering about some of these things. Our purpose here is to suggest effective methods of advance study and to describe civil service examinations.

Your chances for success on this examination can be increased if you know how to prepare. Those "pre-examination jitters" can be reduced if you know what to expect. You can even experience an adventure in good citizenship if you know why civil service exams are given.

B. *WHY ARE CIVIL SERVICE EXAMINATIONS GIVEN?*

Civil service examinations are important to you in two ways. As a citizen, you want public jobs filled by employees who know how to do their work. As a job seeker, you want a fair chance to compete for that job on an equal footing with other candidates. The best-known means of accomplishing this two-fold goal is the competitive examination.

Exams are widely publicized throughout the nation. They may be administered for jobs in federal, state, city, municipal, town or village governments or agencies.

Any citizen may apply, with some limitations, such as the age or residence of applicants. Your experience and education may be reviewed to see whether you meet the requirements for the particular examination. When these requirements exist, they are reasonable and applied consistently to all applicants. Thus, a competitive examination may cause you some uneasiness now, but it is your privilege and safeguard.

C. *HOW ARE CIVIL SERVICE EXAMS DEVELOPED?*

Examinations are carefully written by trained technicians who are specialists in the field known as "psychological measurement," in consultation with recognized authorities in the field of work that the test will cover. These experts recommend the subject matter areas or skills to be tested; only those knowledges or skills important to your success on the job are included. The most reliable books and source materials available are used as references. Together, the experts and technicians judge the difficulty level of the questions.

Test technicians know how to phrase questions so that the problem is clearly stated. Their ethics do not permit "trick" or "catch" questions. Questions may have been tried out on sample groups, or subjected to statistical analysis, to determine their usefulness.

Written tests are often used in combination with performance tests, ratings of training and experience, and oral interviews. All of these measures combine to form the best-known means of finding the right person for the right job.

II. HOW TO PASS THE WRITTEN TEST

A. *NATURE OF THE EXAMINATION*

To prepare intelligently for civil service examinations, you should know how they differ from school examinations you have taken. In school you were assigned certain definite pages to read or subjects to cover. The examination questions were quite detailed and usually emphasized memory. Civil service exams, on the other hand, try to discover your present ability to perform the duties of a position, plus your potentiality to learn these duties. In other words, a civil service exam attempts to predict how successful you will be. Questions cover such a broad area that they cannot be as minute and detailed as school exam questions.

In the public service similar kinds of work, or positions, are grouped together in one "class." This process is known as *position-classification*. All the positions in a class are paid according to the salary range for that class. One class title covers all of these positions, and they are all tested by the same examination.

B. *FOUR BASIC STEPS*

1) Study the announcement

How, then, can you know what subjects to study? Our best answer is: "Learn as much as possible about the class of positions for which you've applied." The exam will test the knowledge, skills and abilities needed to do the work.

Your most valuable source of information about the position you want is the official exam announcement. This announcement lists the training and experience qualifications. Check these standards and apply only if you come reasonably close to meeting them.

The brief description of the position in the examination announcement offers some clues to the subjects which will be tested. Think about the job itself. Review the duties in your mind. Can you perform them, or are there some in which you are rusty? Fill in the blank spots in your preparation.

Many jurisdictions preview the written test in the exam announcement by including a section called "Knowledge and Abilities Required," "Scope of the Examination," or some similar heading. Here you will find out specifically what fields will be tested.

2) Review your own background

Once you learn in general what the position is all about, and what you need to know to do the work, ask yourself which subjects you already know fairly well and which need improvement. You may wonder whether to concentrate on improving your strong areas or on building some background in your fields of weakness. When the announcement has specified "some knowledge" or "considerable knowledge," or has used adjectives like "beginning principles of..." or "advanced ... methods," you can get a clue as to the number and difficulty of questions to be asked in any given field. More questions, and hence broader coverage, would be included for those subjects which are more important in the work. Now weigh your strengths and weaknesses against the job requirements and prepare accordingly.

3) Determine the level of the position

Another way to tell how intensively you should prepare is to understand the level of the job for which you are applying. Is it the entering level? In other words, is this the position in which beginners in a field of work are hired? Or is it an intermediate or advanced level? Sometimes this is indicated by such words as "Junior" or "Senior" in the class title. Other jurisdictions use Roman numerals to designate the level – Clerk I, Clerk II, for example. The word "Supervisor" sometimes appears in the title. If the level is not indicated by the title, check the description of duties. Will you be working under very close supervision, or will you have responsibility for independent decisions in this work?

4) Choose appropriate study materials

Now that you know the subjects to be examined and the relative amount of each subject to be covered, you can choose suitable study materials. For beginning level jobs, or even advanced ones, if you have a pronounced weakness in some aspect of your training, read a modern, standard textbook in that field. Be sure it is up to date and has general coverage. Such books are normally available at your library, and the librarian will be glad to help you locate one. For entry-level positions, questions of appropriate difficulty are chosen – neither highly advanced questions, nor those too simple. Such questions require careful thought but not advanced training.

If the position for which you are applying is technical or advanced, you will read more advanced, specialized material. If you are already familiar with the basic principles of your field, elementary textbooks would waste your time. Concentrate on advanced textbooks and technical periodicals. Think through the concepts and review difficult problems in your field.

These are all general sources. You can get more ideas on your own initiative, following these leads. For example, training manuals and publications of the government agency which employs workers in your field can be useful, particularly for technical and professional positions. A letter or visit to the government department involved may result in more specific study suggestions, and certainly will provide you with a more definite idea of the exact nature of the position you are seeking.

III. KINDS OF TESTS

Tests are used for purposes other than measuring knowledge and ability to perform specified duties. For some positions, it is equally important to test ability to make adjustments to new situations or to profit from training. In others, basic mental abilities not dependent on information are essential. Questions which test these things may not appear as pertinent to the duties of the position as those which test for knowledge and information. Yet they are often highly important parts of a fair examination. For very general questions, it is almost impossible to help you direct your study efforts. What we can do is to point out some of the more common of these general abilities needed in public service positions and describe some typical questions.

1) General information

Broad, general information has been found useful for predicting job success in some kinds of work. This is tested in a variety of ways, from vocabulary lists to questions about current events. Basic background in some field of work, such as sociology or economics, may be sampled in a group of questions. Often these are principles which have become familiar to most persons through exposure rather than through formal training. It is difficult to advise you how to study for these questions; being alert to the world around you is our best suggestion.

2) Verbal ability

An example of an ability needed in many positions is verbal or language ability. Verbal ability is, in brief, the ability to use and understand words. Vocabulary and grammar tests are typical measures of this ability. Reading comprehension or paragraph interpretation questions are common in many kinds of civil service tests. You are given a paragraph of written material and asked to find its central meaning.

3) Numerical ability

Number skills can be tested by the familiar arithmetic problem, by checking paired lists of numbers to see which are alike and which are different, or by interpreting charts and graphs. In the latter test, a graph may be printed in the test booklet which you are asked to use as the basis for answering questions.

4) Observation

A popular test for law-enforcement positions is the observation test. A picture is shown to you for several minutes, then taken away. Questions about the picture test your ability to observe both details and larger elements.

5) Following directions

In many positions in the public service, the employee must be able to carry out written instructions dependably and accurately. You may be given a chart with several columns, each column listing a variety of information. The questions require you to carry out directions involving the information given in the chart.

6) Skills and aptitudes

Performance tests effectively measure some manual skills and aptitudes. When the skill is one in which you are trained, such as typing or shorthand, you can practice. These tests are often very much like those given in business school or high school courses. For many of the other skills and aptitudes, however, no short-time preparation can be made. Skills and abilities natural to you or that you have developed throughout your lifetime are being tested.

Many of the general questions just described provide all the data needed to answer the questions and ask you to use your reasoning ability to find the answers. Your best preparation for these tests, as well as for tests of facts and ideas, is to be at your physical and mental best. You, no doubt, have your own methods of getting into an exam-taking mood and keeping "in shape." The next section lists some ideas on this subject.

IV. KINDS OF QUESTIONS

Only rarely is the "essay" question, which you answer in narrative form, used in civil service tests. Civil service tests are usually of the short-answer type. Full instructions for answering these questions will be given to you at the examination. But in case this is your first experience with short-answer questions and separate answer sheets, here is what you need to know:

1) Multiple-choice Questions

Most popular of the short-answer questions is the "multiple choice" or "best answer" question. It can be used, for example, to test for factual knowledge, ability to solve problems or judgment in meeting situations found at work.

A multiple-choice question is normally one of three types—

- It can begin with an incomplete statement followed by several possible endings. You are to find the one ending which *best* completes the statement, although some of the others may not be entirely wrong.
- It can also be a complete statement in the form of a question which is answered by choosing one of the statements listed.
- It can be in the form of a problem – again you select the best answer.

Here is an example of a multiple-choice question with a discussion which should give you some clues as to the method for choosing the right answer:

When an employee has a complaint about his assignment, the action which will *best* help him overcome his difficulty is to
- A. discuss his difficulty with his coworkers
- B. take the problem to the head of the organization
- C. take the problem to the person who gave him the assignment
- D. say nothing to anyone about his complaint

In answering this question, you should study each of the choices to find which is best. Consider choice "A" – Certainly an employee may discuss his complaint with fellow employees, but no change or improvement can result, and the complaint remains unresolved. Choice "B" is a poor choice since the head of the organization probably does not know what assignment you have been given, and taking your problem to him is known as "going over the head" of the supervisor. The supervisor, or person who made the assignment, is the person who can clarify it or correct any injustice. Choice "C" is, therefore, correct. To say nothing, as in choice "D," is unwise. Supervisors have and interest in knowing the problems employees are facing, and the employee is seeking a solution to his problem.

2) True/False Questions

The "true/false" or "right/wrong" form of question is sometimes used. Here a complete statement is given. Your job is to decide whether the statement is right or wrong.

SAMPLE: A roaming cell-phone call to a nearby city costs less than a non-roaming call to a distant city.

This statement is wrong, or false, since roaming calls are more expensive.

This is not a complete list of all possible question forms, although most of the others are variations of these common types. You will always get complete directions for answering questions. Be sure you understand *how* to mark your answers – ask questions until you do.

V. RECORDING YOUR ANSWERS

Computer terminals are used more and more today for many different kinds of exams.

For an examination with very few applicants, you may be told to record your answers in the test booklet itself. Separate answer sheets are much more common. If this separate answer sheet is to be scored by machine – and this is often the case – it is highly important that you mark your answers correctly in order to get credit.

An electronic scoring machine is often used in civil service offices because of the speed with which papers can be scored. Machine-scored answer sheets must be marked with a pencil, which will be given to you. This pencil has a high graphite content which responds to the electronic scoring machine. As a matter of fact, stray dots may register as answers, so do not let your pencil rest on the answer sheet while you are pondering the correct answer. Also, if your pencil lead breaks or is otherwise defective, ask for another.

Since the answer sheet will be dropped in a slot in the scoring machine, be careful not to bend the corners or get the paper crumpled.

The answer sheet normally has five vertical columns of numbers, with 30 numbers to a column. These numbers correspond to the question numbers in your test booklet. After each number, going across the page are four or five pairs of dotted lines. These short dotted lines have small letters or numbers above them. The first two pairs may also have a "T" or "F" above the letters. This indicates that the first two pairs only are to be used if the questions are of the true-false type. If the questions are multiple choice, disregard the "T" and "F" and pay attention only to the small letters or numbers.

Answer your questions in the manner of the sample that follows:

32. The largest city in the United States is
    A. Washington, D.C.
    B. New York City
    C. Chicago
    D. Detroit
    E. San Francisco

1) Choose the answer you think is best. (New York City is the largest, so "B" is correct.)
2) Find the row of dotted lines numbered the same as the question you are answering. (Find row number 32)
3) Find the pair of dotted lines corresponding to the answer. (Find the pair of lines under the mark "B.")
4) Make a solid black mark between the dotted lines.

VI. BEFORE THE TEST

Common sense will help you find procedures to follow to get ready for an examination. Too many of us, however, overlook these sensible measures. Indeed, nervousness and fatigue have been found to be the most serious reasons why applicants fail to do their best on civil service tests. Here is a list of reminders:

- Begin your preparation early – Don't wait until the last minute to go scurrying around for books and materials or to find out what the position is all about.
- Prepare continuously – An hour a night for a week is better than an all-night cram session. This has been definitely established. What is more, a night a week for a month will return better dividends than crowding your study into a shorter period of time.
- Locate the place of the exam – You have been sent a notice telling you when and where to report for the examination. If the location is in a different town or otherwise unfamiliar to you, it would be well to inquire the best route and learn something about the building.
- Relax the night before the test – Allow your mind to rest. Do not study at all that night. Plan some mild recreation or diversion; then go to bed early and get a good night's sleep.
- Get up early enough to make a leisurely trip to the place for the test – This way unforeseen events, traffic snarls, unfamiliar buildings, etc. will not upset you.
- Dress comfortably – A written test is not a fashion show. You will be known by number and not by name, so wear something comfortable.
- Leave excess paraphernalia at home – Shopping bags and odd bundles will get in your way. You need bring only the items mentioned in the official notice you received; usually everything you need is provided. Do not bring reference books to the exam. They will only confuse those last minutes and be taken away from you when in the test room.
- Arrive somewhat ahead of time – If because of transportation schedules you must get there very early, bring a newspaper or magazine to take your mind off yourself while waiting.
- Locate the examination room – When you have found the proper room, you will be directed to the seat or part of the room where you will sit. Sometimes you are given a sheet of instructions to read while you are waiting. Do not fill out any forms until you are told to do so; just read them and be prepared.
- Relax and prepare to listen to the instructions
- If you have any physical problem that may keep you from doing your best, be sure to tell the test administrator. If you are sick or in poor health, you really cannot do your best on the exam. You can come back and take the test some other time.

VII. AT THE TEST

The day of the test is here and you have the test booklet in your hand. The temptation to get going is very strong. Caution! There is more to success than knowing the right answers. You must know how to identify your papers and understand variations in the type of short-answer question used in this particular examination. Follow these suggestions for maximum results from your efforts:

1) Cooperate with the monitor

The test administrator has a duty to create a situation in which you can be as much at ease as possible. He will give instructions, tell you when to begin, check to see that you are marking your answer sheet correctly, and so on. He is not there to guard you, although he will see that your competitors do not take unfair advantage. He wants to help you do your best.

2) Listen to all instructions

Don't jump the gun! Wait until you understand all directions. In most civil service tests you get more time than you need to answer the questions. So don't be in a hurry. Read each word of instructions until you clearly understand the meaning. Study the examples, listen to all announcements and follow directions. Ask questions if you do not understand what to do.

3) Identify your papers

Civil service exams are usually identified by number only. You will be assigned a number; you must not put your name on your test papers. Be sure to copy your number correctly. Since more than one exam may be given, copy your exact examination title.

4) Plan your time

Unless you are told that a test is a "speed" or "rate of work" test, speed itself is usually not important. Time enough to answer all the questions will be provided, but this does not mean that you have all day. An overall time limit has been set. Divide the total time (in minutes) by the number of questions to determine the approximate time you have for each question.

5) Do not linger over difficult questions

If you come across a difficult question, mark it with a paper clip (useful to have along) and come back to it when you have been through the booklet. One caution if you do this – be sure to skip a number on your answer sheet as well. Check often to be sure that you have not lost your place and that you are marking in the row numbered the same as the question you are answering.

6) Read the questions

Be sure you know what the question asks! Many capable people are unsuccessful because they failed to *read* the questions correctly.

7) Answer all questions

Unless you have been instructed that a penalty will be deducted for incorrect answers, it is better to guess than to omit a question.

8) Speed tests

It is often better NOT to guess on speed tests. It has been found that on timed tests people are tempted to spend the last few seconds before time is called in marking answers at random – without even reading them – in the hope of picking up a few extra points. To discourage this practice, the instructions may warn you that your score will be "corrected" for guessing. That is, a penalty will be applied. The incorrect answers will be deducted from the correct ones, or some other penalty formula will be used.

9) Review your answers

If you finish before time is called, go back to the questions you guessed or omitted to give them further thought. Review other answers if you have time.

10) Return your test materials

If you are ready to leave before others have finished or time is called, take ALL your materials to the monitor and leave quietly. Never take any test material with you. The monitor can discover whose papers are not complete, and taking a test booklet may be grounds for disqualification.

VIII. EXAMINATION TECHNIQUES

1) Read the general instructions carefully. These are usually printed on the first page of the exam booklet. As a rule, these instructions refer to the timing of the examination; the fact that you should not start work until the signal and must stop work at a signal, etc. If there are any *special* instructions, such as a choice of questions to be answered, make sure that you note this instruction carefully.

2) When you are ready to start work on the examination, that is as soon as the signal has been given, read the instructions to each question booklet, underline any key words or phrases, such as *least, best, outline, describe* and the like. In this way you will tend to answer as requested rather than discover on reviewing your paper that you *listed without describing*, that you selected the *worst* choice rather than the *best* choice, etc.

3) If the examination is of the objective or multiple-choice type – that is, each question will also give a series of possible answers: A, B, C or D, and you are called upon to select the best answer and write the letter next to that answer on your answer paper – it is advisable to start answering each question in turn. There may be anywhere from 50 to 100 such questions in the three or four hours allotted and you can see how much time would be taken if you read through all the questions before beginning to answer any. Furthermore, if you come across a question or group of questions which you know would be difficult to answer, it would undoubtedly affect your handling of all the other questions.

4) If the examination is of the essay type and contains but a few questions, it is a moot point as to whether you should read all the questions before starting to answer any one. Of course, if you are given a choice – say five out of seven and the like – then it is essential to read all the questions so you can eliminate the two that are most difficult. If, however, you are asked to answer all the questions, there may be danger in trying to answer the easiest one first because you may find that you will spend too much time on it. The best technique is to answer the first question, then proceed to the second, etc.

5) Time your answers. Before the exam begins, write down the time it started, then add the time allowed for the examination and write down the time it must be completed, then divide the time available somewhat as follows:

- If 3-1/2 hours are allowed, that would be 210 minutes. If you have 80 objective-type questions, that would be an average of 2-1/2 minutes per question. Allow yourself no more than 2 minutes per question, or a total of 160 minutes, which will permit about 50 minutes to review.
- If for the time allotment of 210 minutes there are 7 essay questions to answer, that would average about 30 minutes a question. Give yourself only 25 minutes per question so that you have about 35 minutes to review.

6) The most important instruction is to *read each question* and make sure you know what is wanted. The second most important instruction is to *time yourself properly* so that you answer every question. The third most important instruction is to *answer every question*. Guess if you have to but include something for each question. Remember that you will receive no credit for a blank and will probably receive some credit if you write something in answer to an essay question. If you guess a letter – say "B" for a multiple-choice question – you may have guessed right. If you leave a blank as an answer to a multiple-choice question, the examiners may respect your feelings but it will not add a point to your score. Some exams may penalize you for wrong answers, so in such cases *only*, you may not want to guess unless you have some basis for your answer.

7) Suggestions
    a. Objective-type questions
        1. Examine the question booklet for proper sequence of pages and questions
        2. Read all instructions carefully
        3. Skip any question which seems too difficult; return to it after all other questions have been answered
        4. Apportion your time properly; do not spend too much time on any single question or group of questions
        5. Note and underline key words – *all, most, fewest, least, best, worst, same, opposite,* etc.
        6. Pay particular attention to negatives
        7. Note unusual option, e.g., unduly long, short, complex, different or similar in content to the body of the question
        8. Observe the use of "hedging" words – *probably, may, most likely,* etc.
        9. Make sure that your answer is put next to the same number as the question
        10. Do not second-guess unless you have good reason to believe the second answer is definitely more correct
        11. Cross out original answer if you decide another answer is more accurate; do not erase until you are ready to hand your paper in
        12. Answer all questions; guess unless instructed otherwise
        13. Leave time for review

    b. Essay questions
        1. Read each question carefully
        2. Determine exactly what is wanted. Underline key words or phrases.
        3. Decide on outline or paragraph answer

4. Include many different points and elements unless asked to develop any one or two points or elements
5. Show impartiality by giving pros and cons unless directed to select one side only
6. Make and write down any assumptions you find necessary to answer the questions
7. Watch your English, grammar, punctuation and choice of words
8. Time your answers; don't crowd material

8) Answering the essay question

Most essay questions can be answered by framing the specific response around several key words or ideas. Here are a few such key words or ideas:

M's: manpower, materials, methods, money, management
P's: purpose, program, policy, plan, procedure, practice, problems, pitfalls, personnel, public relations

   a. Six basic steps in handling problems:
      1. Preliminary plan and background development
      2. Collect information, data and facts
      3. Analyze and interpret information, data and facts
      4. Analyze and develop solutions as well as make recommendations
      5. Prepare report and sell recommendations
      6. Install recommendations and follow up effectiveness

   b. Pitfalls to avoid
      1. *Taking things for granted* – A statement of the situation does not necessarily imply that each of the elements is necessarily true; for example, a complaint may be invalid and biased so that all that can be taken for granted is that a complaint has been registered
      2. *Considering only one side of a situation* – Wherever possible, indicate several alternatives and then point out the reasons you selected the best one
      3. *Failing to indicate follow up* – Whenever your answer indicates action on your part, make certain that you will take proper follow-up action to see how successful your recommendations, procedures or actions turn out to be
      4. *Taking too long in answering any single question* – Remember to time your answers properly

IX. AFTER THE TEST

Scoring procedures differ in detail among civil service jurisdictions although the general principles are the same. Whether the papers are hand-scored or graded by machine we have described, they are nearly always graded by number. That is, the person who marks the paper knows only the number – never the name – of the applicant. Not until all the papers have been graded will they be matched with names. If other tests, such as training and experience or oral interview ratings have been given, scores will be combined. Different parts of the examination usually have different weights. For example, the written test might count 60 percent of the final grade, and a rating of training and experience 40 percent. In many jurisdictions, veterans will have a certain number of points added to their grades.

After the final grade has been determined, the names are placed in grade order and an eligible list is established. There are various methods for resolving ties between those who get the same final grade – probably the most common is to place first the name of the person whose application was received first. Job offers are made from the eligible list in the order the names appear on it. You will be notified of your grade and your rank as soon as all these computations have been made. This will be done as rapidly as possible.

People who are found to meet the requirements in the announcement are called "eligibles." Their names are put on a list of eligible candidates. An eligible's chances of getting a job depend on how high he stands on this list and how fast agencies are filling jobs from the list.

When a job is to be filled from a list of eligibles, the agency asks for the names of people on the list of eligibles for that job. When the civil service commission receives this request, it sends to the agency the names of the three people highest on this list. Or, if the job to be filled has specialized requirements, the office sends the agency the names of the top three persons who meet these requirements from the general list.

The appointing officer makes a choice from among the three people whose names were sent to him. If the selected person accepts the appointment, the names of the others are put back on the list to be considered for future openings.

That is the rule in hiring from all kinds of eligible lists, whether they are for typist, carpenter, chemist, or something else. For every vacancy, the appointing officer has his choice of any one of the top three eligibles on the list. This explains why the person whose name is on top of the list sometimes does not get an appointment when some of the persons lower on the list do. If the appointing officer chooses the second or third eligible, the No. 1 eligible does not get a job at once, but stays on the list until he is appointed or the list is terminated.

X. HOW TO PASS THE INTERVIEW TEST

The examination for which you applied requires an oral interview test. You have already taken the written test and you are now being called for the interview test – the final part of the formal examination.

You may think that it is not possible to prepare for an interview test and that there are no procedures to follow during an interview. Our purpose is to point out some things you can do in advance that will help you and some good rules to follow and pitfalls to avoid while you are being interviewed.

What is an interview supposed to test?

The written examination is designed to test the technical knowledge and competence of the candidate; the oral is designed to evaluate intangible qualities, not readily measured otherwise, and to establish a list showing the relative fitness of each candidate – as measured against his competitors – for the position sought. Scoring is not on the basis of "right" and "wrong," but on a sliding scale of values ranging from "not passable" to "outstanding." As a matter of fact, it is possible to achieve a relatively low score without a single "incorrect" answer because of evident weakness in the qualities being measured.

Occasionally, an examination may consist entirely of an oral test – either an individual or a group oral. In such cases, information is sought concerning the technical knowledges and abilities of the candidate, since there has been no written examination for this purpose. More commonly, however, an oral test is used to supplement a written examination.

Who conducts interviews?

The composition of oral boards varies among different jurisdictions. In nearly all, a representative of the personnel department serves as chairman. One of the members of the board may be a representative of the department in which the candidate would work. In some cases, "outside experts" are used, and, frequently, a businessman or some other representative of the general public is asked to serve. Labor and management or other special groups may be represented. The aim is to secure the services of experts in the appropriate field.

However the board is composed, it is a good idea (and not at all improper or unethical) to ascertain in advance of the interview who the members are and what groups they represent. When you are introduced to them, you will have some idea of their backgrounds and interests, and at least you will not stutter and stammer over their names.

What should be done before the interview?

While knowledge about the board members is useful and takes some of the surprise element out of the interview, there is other preparation which is more substantive. It *is* possible to prepare for an oral interview – in several ways:

1) Keep a copy of your application and review it carefully before the interview

This may be the only document before the oral board, and the starting point of the interview. Know what education and experience you have listed there, and the sequence and dates of all of it. Sometimes the board will ask you to review the highlights of your experience for them; you should not have to hem and haw doing it.

2) Study the class specification and the examination announcement

Usually, the oral board has one or both of these to guide them. The qualities, characteristics or knowledges required by the position sought are stated in these documents. They offer valuable clues as to the nature of the oral interview. For example, if the job involves supervisory responsibilities, the announcement will usually indicate that knowledge of modern supervisory methods and the qualifications of the candidate as a supervisor will be tested. If so, you can expect such questions, frequently in the form of a hypothetical situation which you are expected to solve. NEVER go into an oral without knowledge of the duties and responsibilities of the job you seek.

3) Think through each qualification required

Try to visualize the kind of questions you would ask if you were a board member. How well could you answer them? Try especially to appraise your own knowledge and background in each area, *measured against the job sought*, and identify any areas in which you are weak. Be critical and realistic – do not flatter yourself.

4) Do some general reading in areas in which you feel you may be weak

For example, if the job involves supervision and your past experience has NOT, some general reading in supervisory methods and practices, particularly in the field of human relations, might be useful. Do NOT study agency procedures or detailed manuals. The oral board will be testing your understanding and capacity, not your memory.

5) Get a good night's sleep and watch your general health and mental attitude

You will want a clear head at the interview. Take care of a cold or any other minor ailment, and of course, no hangovers.

What should be done on the day of the interview?

Now comes the day of the interview itself. Give yourself plenty of time to get there. Plan to arrive somewhat ahead of the scheduled time, particularly if your appointment is in the fore part of the day. If a previous candidate fails to appear, the board might be ready for you a bit early. By early afternoon an oral board is almost invariably behind schedule if there are many candidates, and you may have to wait. Take along a book or magazine to read, or your application to review, but leave any extraneous material in the waiting room when you go in for your interview. In any event, relax and compose yourself.

The matter of dress is important. The board is forming impressions about you – from your experience, your manners, your attitude, and your appearance. Give your personal appearance careful attention. Dress your best, but not your flashiest. Choose conservative, appropriate clothing, and be sure it is immaculate. This is a business interview, and your appearance should indicate that you regard it as such. Besides, being well groomed and properly dressed will help boost your confidence.

Sooner or later, someone will call your name and escort you into the interview room. *This is it.* From here on you are on your own. It is too late for any more preparation. But remember, you asked for this opportunity to prove your fitness, and you are here because your request was granted.

What happens when you go in?

The usual sequence of events will be as follows: The clerk (who is often the board stenographer) will introduce you to the chairman of the oral board, who will introduce you to the other members of the board. Acknowledge the introductions before you sit down. Do not be surprised if you find a microphone facing you or a stenotypist sitting by. Oral interviews are usually recorded in the event of an appeal or other review.

Usually the chairman of the board will open the interview by reviewing the highlights of your education and work experience from your application – primarily for the benefit of the other members of the board, as well as to get the material into the record. Do not interrupt or comment unless there is an error or significant misinterpretation; if that is the case, do not hesitate. But do not quibble about insignificant matters. Also, he will usually ask you some question about your education, experience or your present job – partly to get you to start talking and to establish the interviewing "rapport." He may start the actual questioning, or turn it over to one of the other members. Frequently, each member undertakes the questioning on a particular area, one in which he is perhaps most competent, so you can expect each member to participate in the examination. Because time is limited, you may also expect some rather abrupt switches in the direction the questioning takes, so do not be upset by it. Normally, a board member will not pursue a single line of questioning unless he discovers a particular strength or weakness.

After each member has participated, the chairman will usually ask whether any member has any further questions, then will ask you if you have anything you wish to add. Unless you are expecting this question, it may floor you. Worse, it may start you off on an extended, extemporaneous speech. The board is not usually seeking more information. The question is principally to offer you a last opportunity to present further qualifications or to indicate that you have nothing to add. So, if you feel that a significant qualification or characteristic has been overlooked, it is proper to point it out in a sentence or so. Do not compliment the board on the thoroughness of their examination – they have been sketchy, and you know it. If you wish, merely say, "No thank you, I have nothing further to add." This is a point where you can "talk yourself out" of a good impression or fail to present an important bit of information. Remember, *you close the interview yourself.*

The chairman will then say, "That is all, Mr. _____, thank you." Do not be startled; the interview is over, and quicker than you think. Thank him, gather your belongings and take your leave. Save your sigh of relief for the other side of the door.

How to put your best foot forward

Throughout this entire process, you may feel that the board individually and collectively is trying to pierce your defenses, seek out your hidden weaknesses and embarrass and confuse you. Actually, this is not true. They are obliged to make an appraisal of your qualifications for the job you are seeking, and they want to see you in your best light. Remember, they must interview all candidates and a non-cooperative candidate may become a failure in spite of their best efforts to bring out his qualifications. Here are 15 suggestions that will help you:

1) Be natural – Keep your attitude confident, not cocky

If you are not confident that you can do the job, do not expect the board to be. Do not apologize for your weaknesses, try to bring out your strong points. The board is interested in a positive, not negative, presentation. Cockiness will antagonize any board member and make him wonder if you are covering up a weakness by a false show of strength.

2) Get comfortable, but don't lounge or sprawl

Sit erectly but not stiffly. A careless posture may lead the board to conclude that you are careless in other things, or at least that you are not impressed by the importance of the occasion. Either conclusion is natural, even if incorrect. Do not fuss with your clothing, a pencil or an ashtray. Your hands may occasionally be useful to emphasize a point; do not let them become a point of distraction.

3) Do not wisecrack or make small talk

This is a serious situation, and your attitude should show that you consider it as such. Further, the time of the board is limited – they do not want to waste it, and neither should you.

4) Do not exaggerate your experience or abilities

In the first place, from information in the application or other interviews and sources, the board may know more about you than you think. Secondly, you probably will not get away with it. An experienced board is rather adept at spotting such a situation, so do not take the chance.

5) If you know a board member, do not make a point of it, yet do not hide it

Certainly you are not fooling him, and probably not the other members of the board. Do not try to take advantage of your acquaintanceship – it will probably do you little good.

6) Do not dominate the interview

Let the board do that. They will give you the clues – do not assume that you have to do all the talking. Realize that the board has a number of questions to ask you, and do not try to take up all the interview time by showing off your extensive knowledge of the answer to the first one.

7) Be attentive

You only have 20 minutes or so, and you should keep your attention at its sharpest throughout. When a member is addressing a problem or question to you, give him your undivided attention. Address your reply principally to him, but do not exclude the other board members.

8) Do not interrupt

A board member may be stating a problem for you to analyze. He will ask you a question when the time comes. Let him state the problem, and wait for the question.

9) Make sure you understand the question

Do not try to answer until you are sure what the question is. If it is not clear, restate it in your own words or ask the board member to clarify it for you. However, do not haggle about minor elements.

10) Reply promptly but not hastily

A common entry on oral board rating sheets is "candidate responded readily," or "candidate hesitated in replies." Respond as promptly and quickly as you can, but do not jump to a hasty, ill-considered answer.

11) Do not be peremptory in your answers

A brief answer is proper – but do not fire your answer back. That is a losing game from your point of view. The board member can probably ask questions much faster than you can answer them.

12) Do not try to create the answer you think the board member wants

He is interested in what kind of mind you have and how it works – not in playing games. Furthermore, he can usually spot this practice and will actually grade you down on it.

13) Do not switch sides in your reply merely to agree with a board member

Frequently, a member will take a contrary position merely to draw you out and to see if you are willing and able to defend your point of view. Do not start a debate, yet do not surrender a good position. If a position is worth taking, it is worth defending.

14) Do not be afraid to admit an error in judgment if you are shown to be wrong

The board knows that you are forced to reply without any opportunity for careful consideration. Your answer may be demonstrably wrong. If so, admit it and get on with the interview.

15) Do not dwell at length on your present job

The opening question may relate to your present assignment. Answer the question but do not go into an extended discussion. You are being examined for a *new* job, not your present one. As a matter of fact, try to phrase ALL your answers in terms of the job for which you are being examined.

Basis of Rating

Probably you will forget most of these "do's" and "don'ts" when you walk into the oral interview room. Even remembering them all will not ensure you a passing grade. Perhaps you did not have the qualifications in the first place. But remembering them will help you to put your best foot forward, without treading on the toes of the board members.

Rumor and popular opinion to the contrary notwithstanding, an oral board wants you to make the best appearance possible. They know you are under pressure – but they also want to see how you respond to it as a guide to what your reaction would be under the pressures of the job you seek. They will be influenced by the degree of poise you display, the personal traits you show and the manner in which you respond.

ABOUT THIS BOOK

This book contains tests divided into Examination Sections. Go through each test, answering every question in the margin. At the end of each test look at the answer key and check your answers. On the ones you got wrong, look at the right answer choice and learn. Do not fill in the answers first. Do not memorize the questions and answers, but understand the answer and principles involved. On your test, the questions will likely be different from the samples. Questions are changed and new ones added. If you understand these past questions you should have success with any changes that arise. Tests may consist of several types of questions. We have additional books on each subject should more study be advisable or necessary for you. Finally, the more you study, the better prepared you will be. This book is intended to be the last thing you study before you walk into the examination room. Prior study of relevant texts is also recommended. NLC publishes some of these in our Fundamental Series. Knowledge and good sense are important factors in passing your exam. Good luck also helps. So now study this Passbook, absorb the material contained within and take that knowledge into the examination. Then do your best to pass that exam.

EXAMINATION SECTION

EXAMINATION SECTION
TEST 1

DIRECTIONS: Each question or incomplete statement is followed by several suggested answers or completions. Select the one that BEST answers the question or completes the statement. *PRINT THE LETTER OF THE CORRECT ANSWER IN THE SPACE AT THE RIGHT.*

Questions 1-4.

DIRECTIONS: Questions 1 through 4 are to be answered on the basis of the following passage.

Those engaged in the exercise of First Amendment rights by pickets, marches, parades, and open-air assemblies are not exempted from obeying valid local traffic ordinances. In a recent pronouncement, Mr. Justice Baxter, speaking for the Supreme Court, wrote:

The rights of free speech and assembly, while fundamental to our democratic society, still do not mean that everyone with opinions or beliefs to express may address a group at any public place and at any time. The constitutional guarantee of liberty implies the existence of an organized society maintaining public order, without which liberty itself would be lost in the excesses of anarchy. The control of travel on the streets is a clear example of governmental responsibility to insure this necessary order. A restriction in that relation, designed to promote the public convenience in the interest of all, and not susceptible to abuses of discriminatory application, cannot be disregarded by the attempted exercise of some civil rights which, in other circumstances, would be entitled to protection. One would not be justified in ignoring the familiar red light because this was thought to be a means of social protest. Governmental authorities have the duty and responsibility to keep their streets open and available for movement. A group of demonstrators could not insist upon the right to cordon off a street, or entrance to a public or private building, and allow no one to pass who did not agree to listen to their exhortations.

1. Which of the following statements BEST reflects Mr. Justice Baxter's view of the relationship between liberty and public order?

   A. Public order cannot exist without liberty.
   B. Liberty cannot exist without public order.
   C. The existence of liberty undermines the existence of public order.
   D. The maintenance of public order insures the existence of liberty.

   1.____

2. According to the above passage, local traffic ordinances result from

   A. governmental limitations on individual liberty
   B. governmental responsibility to insure public order
   C. majority rule as determined by democratic procedures
   D. restrictions on expression of dissent

   2.____

3. The foregoing passage suggests that government would be acting IMPROPERLY if a local traffic ordinance

   A. was enforced in a discriminatory manner
   B. resulted in public inconvenience

   3.____

1

    C.   violated the right of free speech and assembly
    D.   was not essential to public order

4.   Of the following, the MOST appropriate title for the above passage is: 4.____

    A.   THE RIGHTS OF FREE SPEECH AND ASSEMBLY
    B.   ENFORCEMENT OF LOCAL TRAFFIC ORDINANCES
    C.   FIRST AMENDMENT RIGHTS AND LOCAL TRAFFIC ORDINANCES
    D.   LIBERTY AND ANARCHY

Questions 5-8.

DIRECTIONS: Questions 5 through 8 are to be answered on the basis of the following passage.

On November 8, 1976, the Supreme Court refused to block the payment of Medicaid funds for elective abortions. The Court's action means that a new Federal statute that bars the use of Federal funds for abortions unless abortion is necessary to save the life of the mother will not go into effect for many months, if at all.

A Federal District Court in Brooklyn ruled the following month that the statute was unconstitutional and ordered that Federal reimbursement for the costs of abortions continue on the same basis as reimbursements for the costs of pregnancy and childbirth-related services.

Technically, what the Court did today was to deny a request by Senator Howard Ramsdell and others for a stay blocking enforcement of the District Court order pending appeal. The Court's action was a victory for New York City. The City's Health and Hospitals Corporation initiated one of the two lawsuits challenging the new statute that led to the District Court's decision. The Corporation also opposed the request for a Supreme Court stay of that decision, telling the Court in a memorandum that a stay would subject the Corporation to a grave and irreparable injury."

5.   According to the above passage, it would be CORRECT to state that the Health and   5.____
Hospitals Corporation

    A.   joined Senator Ramsdell in his request for a stay
    B.   opposed the statute which limited reimbursement for the cost of abortions
    C.   claimed that it would experience a loss if the District Court order was enforced
    D.   appealed the District Court decision

6.   The above passage indicates that the Supreme Court acted in DIRECT response to   6.____

    A.   a lawsuit initiated by the Health and Hospitals Corporation
    B.   a ruling by a Federal District Court
    C.   a request for a stay
    D.   the passage of a new Federal statute

7.   According to the above passage, it would be CORRECT to state that the Supreme Court   7.____

    A.   blocked enforcement of the District Court order
    B.   refused a request for a stay to block enforcement of the Federal statute
    C.   ruled that the new Federal statute was unconstitutional
    D.   permitted payment of Federal funds for abortion to continue

8. Following are three statements concerning abortion that might be correct: 8.____
    I. Abortion costs are no longer to be Federally reimbursed on the same basis as those for pregnancy and childbirth
    II. Federal funds have not been available for abortions except to save the life of the mother
    III. Medicaid has paid for elective abortions in the past

    According to the passage given above, which of the following CORRECTLY classifies the above statements into those that are true and those that are not true?

    A. I is true, but II and III are not.
    B. I and III are true, but II is not.
    C. I and II are true, but III is not.
    D. III is true, but I and II are not.

9. A legal memorandum will often include the following six sections: 9.____
    I. Conclusions
    II. Issues
    III. Analysis
    IV. Facts
    V. Unknowns
    VI. Counter-analysis

    Which of the following choices lists these sections in the sequence that is generally MOST appropriate for a legal memorandum?

    A. III, VI, IV, V, II, I   B. IV, II, III, VI, I, V
    C. V, II, IV, III, VI, I   D. II, IV, V, III, I, VI

Questions 10-13.

DIRECTIONS: Questions 10 through 13 consist of two sentences each. The sentences deal with the use of court opinions and cases in the writing of legal memoranda. Select answer
      A. if only sentence I is correct
      B. if only sentence II is correct
      C. if both sentences are correct
      D. if neither sentence is correct

10.   I. State the issues in the case as narrowly and precisely as possible.   10.____
     II. Quote frequently and at great length from the court opinions.

11.   I. Describe briefly the issues in the case that are not related to your problem.   11.____
     II. Do not mention discrepancies between the facts of the case and the facts of your problem.

12.   I. Do not refer to the holding or ruling in the case if it is harmful to your client.   12.____
     II. If the holding or ruling in the case is beneficial to your client, try to show that the facts of your problem are analogous to the facts of the case.

13. I. After stating your position concerning the issues and facts, present the opposite   13._____
         viewpoint as effectively as you can.
    II. Avoid stating your own opinions or conclusions concerning the applicability of the
         case.

14. Column V lists four publications in the legal field. Column W contains descriptions of   14._____
     basic subject matter of legal publications.
     Select the one of the following choices which BEST matches the publications in Col-
     umn V with the subject matter in Column W.

Column V	Column W
I. Harvard Law Review	1. Law
II. Supreme Court Reporter	2. Commentary on law
III. McKinney's Consolidated	3. Combination of lawand com
Laws of New York mentary	
IV. The Criminal Law Reporter	

A. I-3; II-1; III-2; IV-3   B. I-2; II-3; III-2; IV-3
C. I-2; II-1; III-3; IV-3   D. I-2; II-3; III-3; IV-1

15. Tickler systems are used in many legal offices for scheduling and calendar control.   15._____
     Of the following, the LEAST common use of a tickler system is to

A. keep papers filed in such a way that they may easily be retrieved
B. arrange for the appearance of witnesses when they will be needed
C. remind lawyers when certain papers are due
D. arrange for the gathering of certain types of evidence

KEY (CORRECT ANSWERS)

1.	B	6.	C
2.	B	7.	D
3.	A	8.	D
4.	C	9.	B
5.	B	10.	A

11.	D
12.	B
13.	A
14.	C
15.	A

TEST 2

DIRECTIONS: Each question or incomplete statement is followed by several suggested answers or completions. Select the one that BEST answers the question or completes the statement. *PRINT THE LETTER OF THE CORRECT ANSWER IN THE SPACE AT THE RIGHT.*

1. Studying the legislative history of a statute by reading the transcript of the hearings that were held on that subject is useful to the legal researcher PRIMARILY because it   1._____

    A. is informative of the manner in which laws are enacted
    B. helps him to understand the intent of the statute
    C. provides leads to statutes on the same subject
    D. clarifies the meaning of other statutes

2. Following are three statements concerning legal research that might be correct: 2._____
    I. The researcher may begin with a particular premise and, in researching it, may discover an entirely new approach to the problem
    II. When the researcher has located a relevant statute, it is not necessary to read court opinions interpreting or applying this statute
    III. A statute which is related to, but not the same as, the point being researched may have notes which will refer the researcher to more relevant cases
    Which of the following ACCURATELY classifies the above statements into those which are correct and those which are not?

    A. II and III are correct, but I is not.
    B. I and III are correct, but II is not.
    C. I and II are correct, but III is not.
    D. I, II, and III are all correct.

3. Of the following, the FIRST action a legal researcher should take in order to locate the laws relevant to a case is to   3._____

    A. search the index of a law book
    B. read statutes on similar subjects to discover pertinent annotations
    C. read a legal digest to become familiar with the law on the subject
    D. prepare a list of descriptive words applicable to the facts of the case

4. Which of the following is the BEST source for a legal researcher to consult in order to find historical data, cross-references, and case excerpts on cases, statutes, and regulations?   4._____

    A. Annotations
    C. Hornbooks
    B. Digests
    D. Casebooks

Questions 5-8.

DIRECTIONS: Each of Questions 5 through 8 contains two sentences concerning criminal law. Some of the sentences contain errors in English grammar or usage. A sentence does not contain an error simply because it could be written in a different manner. For each question, choose answer
    A. if only sentence I is correct
    B. if only sentence II is correct
    C. if both sentences are correct
    D. if neither sentence is correct

5. I. Limiting the term *property* to tangible property, in the criminal mischief setting, accords with prior case law holding that only tangible property came within the purview of the offense of malicious mischief.
   II. Thus, a person who intentionally destroys the property of another, but under an honest belief that he has title to such property, cannot be convicted of criminal mischief under the Revised Penal Law.

   5.____

6. I. Very early in it's history, New York enacted statutes from time to time punishing, either as a felony or as a misdemeanor, malicious injuries to various kinds of property: piers, booms, dams, bridges, etc.
   II. The application of the statute is necessarily restricted to trespassory takings with larcenous intent: namely with intent permanently or virtually permanently to *appropriate* property or *deprive* the owner of its use.

   6.____

7. I. Since the former Penal Law did not define the instruments of forgery in a general fashion, its crime of forgery was held to be narrower than the common law offense in this respect and to embrace only those instruments explicitly specified in the substantive provisions.
   II. After entering the barn through an open door for the purpose of stealing, it was closed by the defendants.

   7.____

8. I. The use of fire or explosives to destroy tangible property is proscribed by the criminal mischief provisions of the Revised Penal Law.
   II. The defendant's taking of a taxicab for the immediate purpose of affecting his escape did not constitute grand larceny

   8.____

Questions 9-13.

DIRECTIONS: Questions 9 through 13 are to be answered SOLELY on the basis of the following passage.

The law is quite clear that evidence obtained in violation of Section 605 of the Federal Communications Act is not admissible in federal court. However, the law as to the admissibility of evidence in state court is far from clear. Had the Supreme Court of the United States made the wiretap exclusionary rule applicable to the states, such confusion would not exist.

In the case of Alton v. Texas, the Supreme Court was called upon to determine whether wiretapping by state and local officers came within the proscription of the federal statute and, if so, whether Section 605 required the same remedies for its vindication in state courts. In answer to the first question, Mr. Justice Minton, speaking for the court, flatly stated that Section 605 made it a federal crime for anyone to intercept telephone messages and divulge what he learned. The court went on to say that a state officer who testified in state court concerning the existence, contents, substance, purport, effect or meaning of an intercepted conversation violated the federal law and committed a criminal act. In regard to the second question, however, the Supreme Court felt constrained by due regard for federal-state relations to answer in the negative. Mr. Justice Minton stated that the court would not presume, in the absence of a clear manifestation of congressional intent, that Congress intended to supersede state rules of evidence.

Because the Supreme Court refused to apply the exclusionary rule to wiretap evidence that was being used in state courts, the states respectively made this decision for themselves. According to hearings held before a congressional committee in 1975, six states authorize wiretapping by statute, 33 states impose total bans on wiretapping, and 11 states have no definite statute on the subject. For examples of extremes, a statute in Pennsylvania will be compared with a statute in New York.

The Pennsylvania statute provides that no communications by telephone or telegraph can be intercepted without permission of both parties. It also specifically prohibits such interception by public officials and provides that evidence obtained cannot be used in court.

The lawmakers in New York, recognizing the need for legal wiretapping, authorized wiretapping by statute. A New York law authorizes the issuance of an ex parte order upon oath or affirmation for limited wiretapping. The aim of the New York law is to allow court-ordered wiretapping and to encourage the testimony of state officers concerning such wiretapping in court. The New York law was found to be constitutional by the New York State Supreme Court in 1975. Other states, including Oregon, Maryland, Nevada, and Massachusetts, enacted similar laws which authorize court-ordered wiretapping.

To add to this legal disarray, the vast majority of the states, including New Jersey and New York, permit wiretapping evidence to be received in court even though obtained in violation of the state laws and of Section 605 of the Federal act. However, some states such as Rhode Island have enacted statutory exclusionary rules which provide that illegally procured wiretap evidence is incompetent in civil as well as criminal actions.

9. According to the above passage, a state officer who testifies in New York State court concerning the contents of a conversation he overheard through a court-ordered wiretap is in violation of _____ law.   9._____

    A. state law but not federal
    B. federal law but not state
    C. federal law and state
    D. neither federal nor state

10. According to the above passage, which of the following statements concerning states statutes on wiretapping is CORRECT?   10._____

    A. The number of states that impose total bans on wiretapping is three times as great as the number of states with no definite statute on wiretapping.
    B. The number of states having no definite statute on wiretapping is more than twice the number of states authorizing wiretapping.
    C. The number of states which authorize wiretapping by statute and the number of states having no definite statute on wiretapping exceed the number of states imposing total bans on wiretapping.
    D. More states authorize wiretapping by statute than impose total bans on wiretapping.

11. Following are three statements concerning wiretapping that might be valid: 11.____
    I.   In Pennsylvania, only public officials may legally intercept telephone communications
    II. In Rhode Island, evidence obtained through an illegal wiretap is incompetent in criminal, but not civil, actions
    III. Neither Massachusetts nor Pennsylvania authorizes wiretapping by public officials

    According to the above passage, which of the following CORRECTLY classifies these statements into those that are valid and those that are not?

    A.   I is valid, but II and III are not.
    B.   II is valid, but I and III are not.
    C.   II and III are valid, but I is not.
    D.   None of the statements is valid.

12. According to the foregoing passage, evidence obtained in violation of Section 605 of the   12.____
    Federal Communications Act is inadmissible in

    A.   federal court but not in any state courts
    B.   federal court and all state courts
    C.   all state courts but not in federal court
    D.   federal court and some state courts

13. In regard to state rules of evidence, Mr. Justice Minton expressed the Court's opinion   13.____
    that Congress

    A.   intended to supersede state rules of evidence, as manifested by Section 605 of the Federal Communications Act
    B.   assumed that federal statutes would govern state rules of evidence in all wiretap cases
    C.   left unclear whether it intended to supersede state rules of evidence
    D.   precluded itself from superseding state rules of evidence through its regard for federal-state relations

14. You begin to ask follow-up questions of a witness who has given a statement. The witness starts to digress before answering an important question satisfactorily.   14.____
    In this situation, the BEST of the following steps is to

    A.   guide the interview by suggesting answers to questions as they are asked
    B.   ask questions which can be answered only with a simple *yes* or *no*
    C.   construct questions as precisely as possible
    D.   tell the witness to keep his answers brief

15. During an interview with a client, you have occasion to refer to a matter which is described in the legal profession by a technical term.   15.____
    Of the following, it would generally be MOST appropriate for you to

    A.   discuss the underlying legal concept in detail
    B.   avoid the subject since it is too complicated
    C.   ask the client if he is familiar with the technical term
    D.   describe the matter in everyday language

KEY (CORRECT ANSWERS)

1. B
2. B
3. D
4. A
5. C

6. B
7. A
8. A
9. B
10. A

11. D
12. D
13. C
14. C
15. D

―――――――

EXAMINATION SECTION
TEST 1

DIRECTIONS: Each question or incomplete statement is followed by several suggested answers or completions. Select the one that BEST answers the question or completes the statement. *PRINT THE LETTER OF THE CORRECT ANSWER IN THE SPACE AT THE RIGHT.*

Questions 1-4.

DIRECTIONS: Questions 1 through 4 consist of sentences concerning criminal law. Some of the sentences contain errors in English grammar or usage, punctuation, spelling or capitalization. A sentence does not contain an error simply because it could be written in a different manner. Choose answer
    A. if the sentence contains an error in English grammar or usage
    B. if the sentence contains an error in punctuation
    C. if the sentence contains an error in spelling or capitalization
    D. if the sentence does not contain any errors

1. The severity of the sentence prescribed by contemporary statutes - including both the former and the revised New York Penal Laws - do not depend on what crime was intended by the offender.   1.____

2. It is generally recognized that two defects in the early law of attempt played a part in the birth of burglary: (1) immunity from prosecution for conduct short of the last act before completion of the crime, and (2) the relatively minor penalty imposed for an attempt (it being a common law misdemeanor) vis-a-vis the completed offense.   2.____

3. The first sentence of the statute is applicable to employees who enter their place of employment, invited guests, and all other persons who have an express or implied license or privilege to enter the premises.   3.____

4. Contemporary criminal codes in the United States generally divide burglary into various degrees, differentiating the categories according to place, time and other attendent circumstances.   4.____

Questions 5-8.

DIRECTIONS: Questions 5 through 8 are to be answered SOLELY on the basis of the following passage.

The difficulty experienced in determining which party has the burden of proving payment or non-payment is due largely to a tack of consistency between the rules of pleading and the rules of proof. In some cases, a plaintiff is obligated by a rule of pleading to allege non-payment on his complaint, yet is not obligated to prove non-payment on the trial. An action upon a contract for the payment of money will serve as an illustration. In such a case, the plaintiff must allege non-payment in his complaint, but the burden of proving payment on the trial is upon the defendant. An important and frequently cited case on this problem is Conkling v. Weatherwax. In that case, the action was brought to establish and enforce a legacy as a lien upon real property. The defendant alleged in her answer that the legacy had been paid. There was no witness competent to testify for the plaintiff to show that the legacy had not been paid. *Therefore, the question of the burden of proof became of primary importance since, if the plaintiff had the burden of proving non-payment, she must fail in her action; whereas, if the burden of proof was on the defendant to prove payment, the plaintiff might win. The Court of Appeals held that the burden of proof was on the plaintiff. In the course of his opinion, Judge Vann attempted to harmonize the conflicting cases on this subject, and for that purpose formulated three rules. These rules have been construed and applied to numerous subsequent cases. As so construed and applied, these may be summarized as follows:*

Rule 1:   *In an action upon a contract for the payment of money only, where the complaint does not allege a balance due over and above all payments made, the plaintiff must allege nonpayment in his complaint, but the burden of proving payment is upon the defendant. In such a case, payment is an affirmative defense which the defendant must plead in his answer. If the defendant fails to plead payment, but pleads a general denial instead, he will not be permitted to introduce evidence of payment.*

Rule 2:   *Where the complaint sets forth a balance in excess of all payments, owing to the structure of the pleading, burden is upon the plaintiff to prove his allegation. In this case, the defendant is not required to plead payment as a defense in his answer but may introduce evidence of payment under a general denial.*

Rule 3:   *When the action is not upon contract for the payment of money, but is upon an obligation created by operation of law, or is for the enforcement of a lien where non-payment of the amount secured is part of the cause of action, it is necessary both to allege and prove the fact of nonpayment.*

5. In the above passage, the case of Conkling v. Weatherwax was cited PRIMARILY to illustrate   5._____

   A. a case where the burden of proof was on the defendant to prove payment
   B. how the question of the burden of proof can affect the outcome of a case
   C. the effect of a legacy as a lien upon real property
   D. how conflicting cases concerning the burden of proof were harmonized

6. According to the above passage, the pleading of payment is a defense in   6._____

   A. Rule 1, but not Rules 2 and 3
   B. Rule 2, but not Rules 1 and 3
   C. Rules 1 and 3, but not Rule 2
   D. Rules 2 and 3, but not Rule 1

7. The facts in Conkling v. Weatherwax closely resemble the conditions described in Rule   7._____

   A. 1   B. 2
   C. 3   D. none of the rules

8. The major topic of the above passage may BEST be described as   8._____

   A. determining the ownership of property
   B. providing a legal definition
   C. placing the burden of proof
   D. formulating rules for deciding cases

Questions 9-12.

DIRECTIONS: Questions 9 through 12 consist of six sentences which can be arranged in a logical sequence. For each question, select the choice which places the numbered sentences in the MOST logical sequence.

9.
I. The burden of proof as to each issue is determined before trial and remains upon the same party throughout the trial.
II. The jury is at liberty to believe one witness testimony as against a number of contradictory witnesses.
III. In a civil case, the party bearing the burden of proof is required to prove his contention by a fair preponderance of the evidence.
IV. However, it must be noted that a fair preponderance of evidence does not necessarily mean a greater number of witnesses.
V. The burden of proof is the burden which rests upon one of the parties to an action to persuade the trier of the facts, generally the jury, that a proposition he asserts is true.
VI. If the evidence is equally balanced, or if it leaves the jury in such doubt as to be unable to decide the controversy either way, judgment must be given against the party upon whom the burden of proof rests.

9._____

The CORRECT sequence is:

A. III, II, V, IV, I, VI
C. III, IV, V, I, II, VI
B. I, II, VI, V, III, IV
D. V, I, III, VI, IV, II

10.
I. If a parent is without assets and is unemployed, he cannot be convicted of the crime of non-support of a child.
II. The term *sufficient ability* has been held to mean sufficient financial ability.
III. It does not matter if his unemployment is by choice or unavoidable circumstances.
IV. If he fails to take any steps at all, he may be liable to prosecution for endangering the welfare of a child.
V. Under the penal law, a parent is responsible for the support of his minor child only if the parent is of sufficient ability.
VI. An indigent parent may meet his obligation by borrowing money or by seeking aid under the provisions of the Social Welfare Law.

10._____

The CORRECT sequence is:

A. VI, I, V, III, II, IV
C. V, II, I, III, VI, IV
B. I, III, V, II, IV, VI
D. I, VI, IV, V, II, III

11.
   I.   Consider, for example, the case of a rabble rouser who urges a group of twenty people to go out and break the windows of a nearby factory.
   II.   Therefore, the law fills the indicated gap with the crime of *inciting to riot.*
   III.   A person is considered guilty of inciting to riot when he urges ten or more persons to engage in tumultuous and violent conduct of a kind likely to create public alarm.
   IV.   However, if he has not obtained the cooperation of at least four people, he cannot be charged with unlawful assembly.
   V.   The charge of inciting to riot was added to the law to cover types of conduct which cannot be classified as either the crime of *riot* or the crime of *unlawful* assembly.
   VI.   If he acquires the acquiescence of at least four of them, he is guilty of unlawful assembly even if the project does not materialize.

11.____

The CORRECT sequence is:

A. III, V, I, VI, IV, II
C. III, IV, I, V, II, VI

B. V, I, IV, VI, II, III
D. V, I, IV, VI, III, II

12.
   I.   If, however, the rebuttal evidence presents an issue of credibility, it is for the jury to determine whether the presumption has, in fact, been destroyed.
   II.   Once sufficient evidence to the contrary is introduced, the presumption disappears from the trial.
   III.   The effect of a presumption is to place the burden upon the adversary to come forward with evidence to rebut the presumption.
   IV.   When a presumption is overcome and ceases to exist in the case, the fact or facts which gave rise to the presumption still remain.
   V.   Whether a presumption has been overcome is ordinarily a question for the court.
   VI.   Such information may furnish a basis for a logical inference.

12.____

The CORRECT sequence is:

A. IV, VI, II, V, I, III
C. V, III, VI, IV, II, I

B. III, II, V, I, IV, VI
D. V, IV, I, II, VI, III

13.   In order to obtain an accurate statement from a person who has witnessed a crime, it is BEST to question the witness

13.____

A. as soon as possible after the crime was committed
B. after the witness has discussed the crime with other witnesses
C. after the witness has had sufficient time to reflect on events and formulate a logical statement
D. after the witness has been advised that he is obligated to tell the whole truth

14.   A young woman was stabbed in the hand in her home by her estranged boyfriend. Her mother and two sisters were at home at the time.
Of the following, it would generally be BEST to interview the young woman in the presence of

14.____

A. her mother only
B. all members of her immediate family
C. members of the family who actually observed the crime
D. the official authorities

15. The one of the following which is NOT effective in obtaining complete testimony from a witness during an interview is to 15.____

    A. ask questions in chronological order
    B. permit the witness to structure the interview
    C. make sure you fully understand the response to each question
    D. review questions to be asked beforehand

_____

KEY (CORRECT ANSWERS)

1.	A	6.	A
2.	D	7.	C
3.	D	8.	C
4.	C	9.	D
5.	B	10.	C

11.	A
12.	B
13.	A
14.	D
15.	B

_____

TEST 2

DIRECTIONS: Each question or incomplete statement is followed by several suggested answers or completions. Select the one that BEST answers the question or completes the statement. *PRINT THE LETTER OF THE CORRECT ANSWER IN THE SPACE AT THE RIGHT.*

1. You are conducting an initial interview with a witness who expresses reluctance, even hostility, to being questioned. You feel it would be helpful to take some notes during the interview.
    In this situation, it would be BEST to

    A. put off note-taking until a follow-up interview and concentrate on establishing rapport with the witness
    B. explain the necessity of note-taking and proceed to take notes during the interview
    C. make notes from memory after the witness has left
    D. take notes, but as unobtrusively as possible

    1.____

2. An assistant is starting an interview with an elderly man who was the victim of a robbery. The man begins by mentioning his minor aches and pains. The aide immediately changes the subject to the robbery.
    This action by the aide should GENERALLY be considered

    A. *proper* chiefly because it speeds up the interviewing process
    B. *improper* chiefly because the man is likely to become confused as to what information is really important
    C. *proper* chiefly because the man is likely to be impressed with the aide's interest in the crime
    D. *improper* chiefly because an opportunity for gaining pertinent information may be lost

    2.____

3. You are interviewing the owner of a stolen car about facts relating to the robbery. After completing his statement, the car owner suddenly states that some of the details he has just related are not correct. You realize that this change might be significant.
    Of the following, it would be BEST for you to

    A. ask the owner what other details he may have given incorrectly
    B. make a note of the discrepancy for discussion at a later date
    C. repeat your questioning on the details that were misstated until you have covered that area completely
    D. explain to the owner that because of his change of testimony, you will have to repeat the entire interview

    3.____

4. You are interviewing a client who has just been assaulted. He has trouble collecting his thoughts and telling his story coherently.
    Which of the following represents the MOST effective method of questioning under these circumstances?

    A. Ask questions which structure the client's story chronologically into units, each with a beginning, middle, and end.
    B. Ask several questions at a time to structure the interview.

    4.____

C. Ask open-ended questions which allow the client to respond in a variety of ways.
D. Begin the interview with several detailed questions in order to focus the client's attention on the situation.

5. Following are two statements that might be correct concerning the relationship with clients:

    I. When practical the client should be encouraged to take some steps on his own behalf to aid the office in handling his case
    II. The client should be told what steps the office proposes to take on his behalf

Which of the following CORRECTLY classifies the above statements?

A. Statement I is generally correct, but Statement II is not.
B. Statement II is generally correct, but Statement I is not.
C. Both statements are generally correct.
D. Neither statement is generally correct.

5._____

6. You are in the District Attorney's office interviewing an elderly female victim of an assault in order to prepare a list of charges.
The one of the following which would be MOST important in determining all the facts is

A. creating a close, cooperative working relationship with the victim
B. establishing your authority at the beginning of the interview
C. maintaining a relaxed atmosphere during the interview
D. having access to the particular statutes which might apply to this case

6._____

7. A client is critical of the way he has been treated by government agencies in the past. A paralegal aide interviewing him defends the overall performance of government employees.
This reaction by the aide is GENERALLY

A. *appropriate;* the aide has an obligation to defend fellow workers in government service when such defense is justified
B. *inappropriate;* the aide should remain neutral rather than volunteer his personal opinions
C. *appropriate;* the aide should honestly express his personal opinions in such circumstances unless it is likely to provoke antagonism
D. *inappropriate;* the aide should agree with the client's comments to help establish a greater rapport with him

7._____

Questions 8-11.

DIRECTIONS: Questions 8 through 11 are to be answered SOLELY on the basis of the following passage.

A person may use physical force upon another person when and to the extent he reasonably believes such to be necessary to defend himself or a third person from what he reasonably believes to be the use or imminent use of unlawful physical force by such other person, unless (a) the latter's conduct was provoked by the actor himself with intent to cause physical injury to another person, or (b) the actor was the initial aggressor; or (c) the physical force involved is the product of a combat by agreement not specifically authorized by law.

A person may not use deadly physical force upon another person under the circumstances specified above unless: (a) he reasonably believes that such other person is using or is about to use deadly physical force. Even in such case, however, the actor may not use deadly physical force if he knows he can with complete safety as to himself and others avoid the necessity of doing so by retreating, except that he is under no duty to retreat if he is in his dwelling and is not the initial aggressor; or (b) he reasonably believes that such other person is committing or attempting to commit a kidnapping, forcible rape, or forcible sodomy.

8. Jones and Smith, who have not met before, get into an argument in a tavern. Smith takes a punch at Jones but misses. Jones then hits Smith on the chin with his fist. Smith falls to the floor and suffers minor injuries. According to the above passage, it would be CORRECT to state that

   A. *only* Smith was justified in using physical force
   B. *only* Jones was justified in using physical force
   C. both Smith and Jones were justified in using physical force
   D. neither Smith nor Jones was justified in using physical force

8._____

9. While walking down the street, Brady observes Miller striking Mrs. Adams on the head with his fist in an attempt to steal her purse.
   According to the above passage, it would be CORRECT to state that Brady would

   A. not be justified in using deadly physical force against Miller since Brady can safety retreat
   B. be justified in using physical force against Miller, but not deadly physical force
   C. not be justified in using physical force against Miller since Brady himself is not being attacked
   D. be justified in using deadly physical force

9._____

10. Winters is attacked from behind by Sharp, who attempts to beat up Winters with a blackjack. Winters disarms Sharp and succeeds in subduing him with a series of blows to the head. Sharp stops fighting and explains that he thought Winters was the person who had robbed his apartment a few minutes before, but now realizes his mistake. According to the above passage, it would be CORRECT to state that

   A. Winters was justified in using physical force on Sharp only to the extent necessary to defend himself
   B. Winters was not justified in using physical force on Sharp since Sharp's attack was provoked by what he believed to be Winters' behavior
   C. Sharp was justified in using physical force on Winters since he reasonably believed that Winters had unlawfully robbed him
   D. Winters was justified in using physical force on Sharp only because Sharp was acting mistakenly in attacking him

10._____

11. Roberts hears a noise in the cellar of his home and, upon investigation, discovers an intruder, Welch. Welch moves towards Roberts in a threatening manner, thrusts his hand into a bulging pocket, and withdraws what appears to be a gun. Roberts thereupon strikes Welch over the head with a golf club. He then sees that the *gun* is a toy. Welch later dies of head injuries.
   According to the above passage, it would be CORRECT to state that Roberts

11._____ .

A. *was justified* in using deadly physical force because he reasonably believed Welch was about to use deadly physical force
B. *was not justified* in using deadly physical force
C. *was justified* in using deadly physical force only because he did not provoke Welch's conduct
D. *was justified* in using deadly physical force only because he was not the initial aggressor

Questions 12-15.

DIRECTIONS: Questions 12 through 15 are to be answered SOLELY on the basis of the following passage.

From the beginning, the Supreme Court has supervised the fairness of trials conducted by the Federal government. But the Constitution, as originally drafted, gave the court no such general authority in state oases. The court's power to deal with state cases comes from the Fourteenth Amendment, which became part of the Constitution in 1868. The crucial provision forbids any state to "deprive any person of life, liberty or property without due process of law."

The guarantee of "due process" would seem, at the least, to require fair procedure in criminal trials. But curiously, the Supreme Court did not speak on the question for many decades. During that time, however, the due process clause was interpreted to bar "unreasonable" state economic regulations, such as minimum wage laws.

In 1915, there came the case of Leo M. Frank, a Georgian convicted of murder in a trial that he contended was dominated by mob hysteria. Historians now agree that there was such hysteria, with overtones of anti-semitism.

The Supreme Court held that it could not look past the findings of the Georgia courts that there had been no mob atmosphere at the trial. Justices Oliver Wendell Holmes and Charles Evans Hughes dissented, arguing that the constitutional guarantee would be "a barren one" if the Federal courts could not make their own inferences from the facts.

In 1923, the case of Moore v. Dempsey involved five Arkansas blacks convicted of murder and sentenced to death in a community so aroused against them that at one point they were saved from lynching only by Federal troops. Witnesses against them were said to have been beaten into testifying.

The court, though not actually setting aside the convictions, directed a lower Federal court to hold a habeas corpus hearing to find out whether the trial had been fair, or whether the whole proceeding had been "a mask — that counsel, jury, and judge were swept to the fatal end by an irresistible wave of public opinion."

12. According to the above passage, the Supreme Court's INITIAL interpretation of the Fourteenth Amendment   12._____

    A. protected state supremacy in economic matters
    B. increased the scope of Federal jurisdiction
    C. required fair procedures in criminal trials
    D. prohibited the enactment of minimum wage laws

13. According to the above passage, the Supreme Court in the Frank case   13.____

    A. denied that there had been mob hysteria at the trial
    B. decided that the guilty verdict was supported by the evidence
    C. declined to question the state court's determination of the facts
    D. found that Leo Frank had not received *due process*

14. According to the above passage, the dissenting judges in the Frank case maintained that   14.____

    A. due process was an empty promise in the circumstances of that case
    B. the Federal courts could not guarantee certain provisions of the Constitution
    C. the Federal courts should not make their own inferences from the facts in state cases
    D. the Supreme Court had rendered the Constitution *barren*

15. Of the following, the MOST appropriate title for the above passage is: 15.____

    A. THE CONDUCT OF FEDERAL TRIALS
    B. THE DEVELOPMENT OF STATES' RIGHTS: 1868-1923
    C. MOORE V. DEMPSEY: A CASE STUDY IN CRIMINAL JUSTICE
    D. DUE PROCESS - THE EVOLUTION OF A CONSTITUTIONAL CORNERSTONE

KEY (CORRECT ANSWERS)

1.	B	6.	A
2.	D	7.	B
3.	C	8.	B
4.	A	9.	B
5.	C	10.	A

11.	A
12.	D
13.	C
14.	A
15.	D

EXAMINATION SECTION
TEST 1

DIRECTIONS: Each question or incomplete statement is followed by several suggested answers or completions. Select the one that BEST answers the question or completes the statement. *PRINT THE LETTER OF THE CORRECT ANSWER IN THE SPACE AT THE RIGHT.*

Questions 1-11.

DIRECTIONS: Questions 1 through 11 are to be answered SOLELY on the basis of the following passage.

KELSEN AND THE PURE THEORY OF LAW

Kelsen is the founder and storm center of a school of juristic theory known from its place of origin as the "Vienna School of Jurisprudence" and from its point of view as the "normative theory of law" and the "pure theory of law." His ideas have met with a great deal of opposition and the polemics have been conducted with so much vehemence and passion that, as Kelsen himself says, there is grave suspicion that the motives on the side of the opposition have not been purely theoretical or scientific. According to Kelsen, his opponents could not forgive him for endeavoring to establish a purely formal science of law and of the state which could not be used as a tool in the service of political interests. His general criticism of the pre- vailing theories is that they are not purely juristic, but political. Jurisprudence has been used as a weapon of defense or attack, with a view to justifying or condemning a form of govern- ment or a legal order. This being the situation, particularly in central Europe, a political motive has been sought in Kelsen's theory also. Fascists have seen in it a defense of democratic lib- eralism; liberals and social democrats have regarded it as paving the way to Fascism. Com- munists find in it capitalistic ideology, while the conservatives accuse it of sheer Bolshevism or concealed anarchism. Its spirit has been compared with that of Catholic Scholasticism, Protestantism, and even atheism. Sure proof, Kelsen says, that it is in reality what it claims to be -- none of these, having, as a pure formal science of law, no political or theological implica- tions.

Kelsen carefully prepares the ground in a discussion of the place of jurisprudence among the sciences. He divides the sciences into natural and normative. The natural sciences deal with "Being" and consist in explaining "Being." To explain natural phenomena means to present them as illustrations of the law of causality. A normative science is one which studies the structure or form of the norm, not its content. It is, therefore, a formal science. A norm is distinguished from a natural law. A natural law states a causal relation between "being" and "being" and thus explains "Being." A norm also states a relation between "being" and "Being." The "Being" in this case is in the majority of instances a human act. But the relation in this case is not one of cause and effect, but one of "ought." The norm establishes a duty; it does not explain. "Being" and "ought" are two primary categories of thought. They cannot be defined and are independent of each other. Neither can be derived from the other.

Attempts have been made, Kelsen points out, to reduce norms to natural law. Thus, it is said that moral norms are in effect precipitates of that which a given society or mankind in general have actually been observing for a long time. Kelsen's answer to this is that while it may be true that, psychologically, long habit has the tendency to create in the human mind a feeling that the act in question ought to be observed, it is a confusion of thought to identify the "ought" category with the habit which produced it.

It has been maintained likewise that the norm: "Thou shalt not lie" is only another way of saying: "Lying has a tendency to destroy social confidence," and the latter is a natural law like the proposition: "Alcohol has a tendency to destroy the nervous system." This too is the result of a confusion between the norm which established the duty and the ground in natural law which prompted moralists to establish the norm. Thus, so far as meaning is concerned, norm and natural law are always different.

Thus, Kelsen distinguishes jurisprudence as a normative science separate and distinct from natural sciences. Although there are many kinds of norms, norms of ethics, aesthetics, grammar, logic, law, Kelsen is primarily interested in legal norms. Kelsen has formulated what he calls the primary legal norm. The primary legal norm has the form of a conditional sentence or a hypothetical judgment: "If A steals, he should be punished." The act of stealing is, therefore, not a violation of a norm; it is precisely in connection with the act of stealing that the legal norm becomes effective. Hence, it is a mistake to regard the law as an expression of what people think, or do, or observe. The normative method is here entirely separate from the explicative, and the jurist is concerned primarily with the normative aspect. To be sure, this is only one aspect of law, and does not enable us to comprehend fully the institution or phenomenon of law. The jurist may and should carry on sociological, psychological, and historical studies of the law, but he should not mix these studies, which are explicative, with the formal -- juristic -- normative. These studies do not constitute a psychological or sociological jurisprudence -- there is no such thing, says Kelsen. They are the psychology or sociology of law or of human conduct in relation to law. The theoretical jurist is not interested in the actual behavior of men, but in the "ought" which the law prescribes. His criteria are purely formal like those of the judge.

Of course, moral as well as legal norms determine an "ought." Kelsen feels that a jurist presupposes a given body of law, be its origin what it may, and as he is not interested in the origin so he is not concerned with its purpose, though there is no doubt that legal norms have been established for a purpose. This purpose, however, has no bearing on the meaning of the concepts based upon the norms. He considers legal concepts purely as formal categories and hence admits only formal elements in his definitions. By way of example, geometry is none the less an important and useful science because it considers only the form of bodies; and the same is true of jurisprudence.

Kelsen feels that his pure theory of law is neither the dogmatic jurisprudence which develops a certain juridical order by studying a group of norms or analyzing a particular rule of law in order to make their meaning more precise, nor the history of law which attempts to study the historical origins of a particular juridical order, nor the comparative law which attempts to compare the contents of various juridical orders, looking for conformity or diversity, in order to arrive at certain juridical types, but that of general jurisprudence. This latter, Kelsen says, is a jurisprudence that does not restrict itself to a particular juridical order or to particular rules. The task of such a jurisprudence, therefore, constitutes the theoretical basis for all other branches of jurisprudence.

1. The normative theory of law is

1.____

22

A. frequently mistaken for a theory called the *pure theory of law*
B. synonymous with the *pure theory of law*
C. the storm center of the Vienna School of Jurisprudence
D. largely polemical

2. Kelsen maintains that the *normative theory*   2.____

   A. is a pure science of law having no political or theological implications
   B. must be understood in order to establish the validity of legal systems in a democracy
   C. is meant to be atheistic since there is no reference to an external moral code
   D. supports several different political positions

3. Which one of the following statements is NOT correct?   3.____

   A. Kelsen believes his attackers are not interested in a purely juristic theory of law.
   B. Kelsen criticizes legal theories which are designed to serve political purposes.
   C. Kelsen believes that most jurisprudential theories are used to justify or attack a given form of government.
   D. Kelsen's theories have been accepted by a wide spectrum of political theorists from left to right.

4. Which of the following is the basis of Kelsen's theory of jurisprudence?   4.____

   A. Pure philosophical models
   B. Differences between natural and normative sciences
   C. A geometric model having axioms and postulates
   D. Sociological concepts

5. According to the passage, it would be CORRECT to state that a normative science   5.____

   A. defines cause and effect
   B. explains natural law
   C. examines *being* and what ought to follow
   D. establishes the interdependency of *being* and *duty*

6. According to the passage, it would be CORRECT to state that natural science   6.____

   A. is one category of normative science
   B. studies the structure and form of the norm
   C. is mistakenly believed to explain natural phenomena
   D. deals with and explains *being*

7. Which one of the following statements concerning norms and natural law is NOT correct?   7.____

   A. The universality of a given standard of conduct indicates that it is a true natural law.
   B. Norms cannot be reduced to natural law since the two are not the same.
   C. The equation of natural law with norms arises from the confusion between things that have been done out of habit and things that ought to be done.
   D. *Thou shalt not lie* is an example of a norm.

8. According to the passage, it would be CORRECT to state that Kelsen's primary legal   8.____
norm

A. is an expression of what people do
B. permits a full comprehension of law as an institution
C. defines an illegal act as the violation of a norm
D. takes the form of a hypothetical judgement

9. According to Kelsen, which one of the following statement is NOT correct?   9.____

A. Jurist is concerned primarily with the normative aspect of law.
B. Sociological and psychological studies of the law do not constitute a separate juris-prudence.
C. The theoretical jurist is concerned with the actual behavior of men in relation to the norms which the law prescribes.
D. The normative and explicative methods are entirely different from each other.

10. A jurist concerned with legal norms considers   10.____

A. legal concepts in terms of purely formal criteria
B. whether the *ought* of the legal category conforms to the *ought* of the moral cate-gory
C. the origins of any given body of law
D. the purpose of a body of law in determining the meaning of concepts based upon its norms

11. According to the passage, it would be CORRECT to state that the pure theory of law   11.____

A. is instrumental in the development of comparative jurisprudential analyses
B. constitutes the theoretical basis for all other branches of jurisprudence
C. establishes a body of dogma for the guidance of jurists
D. clarifies the meaning of particular rules of law

12. Trees which grow annually on reality are considered   12.____

A. real property   B. personal property
C. accretions   D. avulsions

13. Where is a grant of a fee simple is to John Jones and Jones, his wife, the grantees take   13.____
as

A. tenants in common   B. individuals
C. joint tenants   D. tenants by the entirety

14. Assume that A and B are joint tenants of realty. A conveys his share of the realty abso-   14.____
lutely to C, without the knowledge or consent of B.
With regard of C's status under these circumstances, it would be CORRECT to state that C

A. becomes a joint tenant with B
B. takes nothing, and A remains a joint tenant with B
C. takes nothing, and A becomes a tenant in common with B
D. becomes a tenant in common with B as to that part of the realty conveyed to him

15. Assume that two persons own a piece of realty as tenants in common. One of them, with-   15.____
out the consent of the other, takes possession of the realty and claims openly to hold
adversely to the other.
Such possession, at its start, is deemed to be

A. adverse possession
B. the possession of the other
C. constructive possession
D. adverse possession only if the property is income-producing

16. Assume that a fee owner conveys a portion of his realty to another, while keeping other land to which he has no access except by passing over the land conveyed. With regard to the grantor's access to the property he retains, it would be CORRECT to state that

    16._____

    A. an easement by prescription inures to the benefit of the grantor
    B. an easement is reserved by implication if at the time of the conveyance it would result in a mere convenience
    C. an easement is reserved by implication if actual necessity exists at the time of the conveyance
    D. no easement exists unless it is stipulated in the instrument conveying the realty

17. Assume that A owns a piece of realty and enters into a valid contract to sell the same to X for a purchase price of $50,000, all cash. Before the closing of title, A dies, leaving a valid will which leaves all of his realty to B and all of his personalty to C. With regard to conveyance of the realty, it would be CORRECT to state that

    17._____

    A. there is no legal duty on anyone's part to execute the conveyance in accordance with the contract
    B. the property must be conveyed with the proceeds going to B
    C. the property must be conveyed with the proceeds going to C
    D. the property must be conveyed with the proceeds shared equally between B and C as a matter of law

18. The statute of limitations in an action on a note which is secured by a mortgage on real property is _____ years.

    18._____

    A. 3   B. 6   C. 10   D. 20

19. Assume that a written lease has been validly assigned by a tenant to an assignee. The lease contains a renewal option in favor of the tenant but is silent as to the rights there to of assignees. With regard to the assignee's rights, it would be CORRECT to state that the

    19._____

    A. assignee may compel the landlord to renew the lease to the assignor
    B. assignment terminated the renewal option
    C. assignee has no rights of any kind with respect to the renewal option
    D. rights of the assignee with respect to the renewal option depend on whether the assignee assumed the obligations of the lease

20. Assume that an employee, after returning home from work, told his wife that he had injured himself on the job that afternoon while lifting some heavy objects. The employee had suffered from chest pains since the lifting incident and thereafter died of a heart attack. The wife subsequently seeks benefits at a Workmen's Compensation hearing. With regard to the admissibility of the employee's statement to his wife at such a hearing, it would be CORRECT to state that the statement is

    20._____

A. inadmissible as a matter of law
B. admissible as a matter of law without regard to any other facts
C. inadmissible solely because of the hearsay rule
D. admissible if corroborated by other evidence

21. Substantial evidence, as required to confirm the finding of an administrative agency on judicial review, is   21.____

    A. evidence beyond a reasonable doubt
    B. such relevant evidence as a reasonable mind might accept as adequate to support a conclusion
    C. a mere scintilla of evidence
    D. a preponderance of the evidence

22. Assume that a municipal contractor is suing the city to recover the balance due on a contract. The contractor had previously been convicted in Federal Court of using interstate facilities with intent to violate the state bribery laws in connection with said contract, and the city counter claims for recovery of the payments already made.
    If there is no basis for determining the damages that the city has sustained, who should recover?   22.____

    A. The contractor is entitled to the balance due.
    B. The city is entitled to recover the payments it has made.
    C. The contractor is entitled to quantum merit.
    D. Neither party is entitled to anything.

23. Assume that the estate of a deceased motorcyclist is bringing an action against a town for negligence in the maintenance of a bridge abutment. The decedent died in an accident when the motorcycle he was driving crashed into the abutment. Immediately after the accident, the coroner ordered an autopsy and blood and urine tests to determine the alcoholic content of the decedent at the time of his death, pursuant to a state statute. Under these circumstances, what action should the court take with regard to the evidence derived from the autopsy and blood and urine tests?
    The court should   23.____

    A. bar the admission of the alcohol analysis into evidence on the grounds that the statute is unconstitutional
    B. allow the defendant town to introduce into evidence that part of the autopsy report which contains the alcohol analysis
    C. bar the admission into evidence by the town that part of the autopsy report which contains the alcohol analysis
    D. allow the alcohol analysis to be introduced in evidence only if the coroner appears to testify

24. Assume that, in a criminal case, a defendant bookseller is charged with possession and sale of an obscene magazine. At the trial, the magazine itself is found to be obscene. Under these circumstances, what presumption, if any, concerning the bookseller's knowledge should apply?   24.____

    A. There is a valid statutory presumption that a seller of obscene materials knows the contents of what he sells.
    B. There is no statutory presumption that a seller of obscene materials knows the contents of what he sells.

C. No presumptions of any kind arise by virtue of the fact that a defendant possessed and sold obscene materials.

D. Actual knowledge of the contents of obscene materials must be proved against the seller.

25. Assume that a plaintiff institutes an action in damages against D and C alleging them to be joint tort feasors whose negligence was the sole cause of his injury, and both D and C appear at the trial.
Under these circumstances, which of the following is a PROPER action for the jury to take?
The jury

    25.____

A. *must,* if it finds for the plaintiff, bring in a single verdict against D and C
B. *can,* if it finds for the plaintiff, exonerate both D and C and bring in a verdict against X, who is not a party to this action
C. *can,* if it finds for the plaintiff, apportion the damages between D and C
D. *can,* if it desires to find for the plaintiff, waive any contributory negligence of the plaintiff but reduce his verdict against D and C

KEY (CORRECT ANSWERS)

1.	B		11.	B
2.	A		12.	A
3.	D		13.	D
4.	B		14.	D
5.	C		15.	B
6.	D		16.	C
7.	A		17.	C
8.	D		18.	B
9.	C		19.	A
10.	A		20.	D

21.	B
22.	B
23.	C
24.	A
25.	C

TEST 2

DIRECTIONS: Each question or incomplete statement is followed by several suggested answers or completions. Select the one that BEST answers the question or completes the statement. *PRINT THE LETTER OF THE CORRECT ANSWER IN THE SPACE AT THE RIGHT.*

Questions 1-10.

DIRECTIONS: Questions 1 through 10 are to be answered SOLELY on the basis of the following sections of the General Business Law.

§200. Safes; limited liability

Whenever the proprietor or manager of any hotel, motel, inn or steamboat shall provide a safe in the office of such hotel, motel or steamboat, or other convenient place for the safe keeping of any money, jewels, ornaments, bank notes, bonds, negotiable securities or precious stones belonging to the guests of or travelers in such hotel, motel, inn or steamboat, and shall notify the guests or travelers thereof by posting a notice stating the fact that such safe is provided, in which such property may be deposited, in a public and conspicuous place and manner in the office and public rooms, and in the public parlors of such hotel, motel, or inn, or saloon of such steam boat, and if such guest or traveller shall neglect to deliver such property, to the person in charge of such office for deposit in such safe, the proprietor or manager of such hotel, motel, or steamboat shall not be liable for any loss of such property, sustained by such guest or traveler by theft or otherwise; but no hotel, motel or steamboat proprietor, manager or lessee shall be obliged to receive property on deposit for safe keeping, exceeding five hundred dollars in value; and if such guest or traveler shall deliver such property to the person in charge of such office for deposit in such safe, said proprietor, manager or lessee shall not be liable for any loss thereof, sustained by such guest or traveler by theft or otherwise, in any sum exceeding the sum of five hundred dollars unless by special agreement in writing with such proprietor, manager or lessee.

§201. Liability for loss of clothing and
other personal property limited

1. No hotel or motel keeper except as provided in the foregoing section shall be liable for damage to or loss of wearing apparel or other personal property in the lobby, hallways or in the room or rooms assigned to a guest for any sum exceeding the sum of five hundred dollars, unless it shall appear that such loss occurred through the fault or negligence of such keeper, nor shall he be liable in any sum exceeding the sum of one hundred dollars for the loss of or damage to any such property when delivered to such keeper for storage or safe keeping in the store room, baggage room or other place elsewhere than in the room or rooms assigned to such guest, unless at the time of delivering the same for storage or safe keeping such value in excess of one hundred dollars shall be stated and a written receipt, stating such value, shall be issued by such keeper, but in no event shall such keeper be liable beyond five hundred dollars, unless it shall appear that such loss occurred through his fault or negligence, and such keeper may make a reasonable charge for storing or keeping such property, nor shall he be liable for the loss of or damage to any merchandise samples or merchandise for sale, unless the guest shall have given such keeper prior written notice of having the same in his possession, together with the value thereof, the receipt of which notice the hotel

or motel keeper shall acknowledge in writing over the signature of himself or his agent, but in no event shall such keeper be liable beyond five hundred dollars, unless it shall appear that such loss or damage occurred through his fault or negligence; as to property deposited by guests or patrons in the parcel or check room of any hotel, motel or restaurant, the delivery of which is evidenced by a check or receipt therefor and for which no fee or charge is exacted, the proprietor shall not be liable beyond seventy-five dollars, unless such value in excess of seventy-five dollars shall be stated upon delivery and a written receipt, stating such value, shall be issued, but he shall in no event be liable beyond one hundred dollars, unless such loss occurs through his fault or negligence. Notwithstanding anything here in above contained, no hotel or motel keeper shall be liable for damage to or loss of such property by fire, when it shall appear that such fire was occasioned without his fault or negligence.

2. A printed copy of this section shall be posted in a conspicuous place and manner in the office or public room and in the public parlors of such hotel or motel.

1. Which one of the following statements concerning Section 200 is NOT correct? 1._____

    A. The section is applicable to hotels, motels and steamboats.
    B. It provides a method whereby the covered places of public accommodation may limit their liability for losses of specified valuables.
    C. It mandates the provision of a safe for the deposit of valuables for all hotels, motels and steamboats.
    D. The provisions of this section apply to the valuables of guests and travelers only.

2. According to the passage, it would be CORRECT to state that if a hotel provides a safe for specified valuables under the conditions specified in Section 200, 2._____

    A. its liability for losses is limited to $500
    B. it may refuse to receive property that is more valuable than $500
    C. its liability is limited to $1,000 unless the guest declares the value to be greater and the manager, proprietor or lessee agrees in writing to accept a higher valuation
    D. it is liable up to a limit of $500 for losses arising only from thefts

3. According to the passage, if a hotel complies with all the requirements of Section 200, and a guest fails to deposit designated valuables in the hotel safe, the guest 3._____

    A. *cannot* hold the public place liable under any circumstances for losses sustained
    B. *can* hold the public place liable only if the property is stolen
    C. *cannot* hold the public place liable unless he can prove the loss occurred through the negligence of the management
    D. *can* hold the management of the public place liable for any loss not in excess of $500

4. Section 201 of the General Business Law establishes the liability of hotels and motels for clothing(,) 4._____

    A. and/or other personal property and valuables stolen from the guest's assigned room
    B. personal property and valuables lost from any cause within the hotel or motel
    C. or personal property, except valuables or merchandise samples or merchandise for sale, which is stolen or otherwise lost
    D. or other personal property, except valuables, lost or stolen from designed areas within the hotel or motel

5. Under Section 201, liability for clothing or other personal property therein designated, with the exception of merchandise, which is lost, stolen or otherwise damaged while in the assigned room is

    A. *limited* to $500 regardless of the cause of the loss
    B. *limited* to $500 if the loss is caused by the management's negligence
    C. *unlimited* under any circumstances
    D. *unlimited* if due to the negligence of the management

5._____

6. Which one of the following provisions is NOT applicable to property that is stored?

    A. The limitations on storage apply only to property stored in storage or baggage rooms and not to property stored in the assigned room.
    B. The limitations on liability for storage areas are applicable only if no storage charge is made.
    C. The hotel or motel is liable in amounts over $100 only if an excess valuation is declared and a written receipt issued.
    D. There is a maximum liability of $500 provided, unless loss is due to the negligence or fault of the management.

6._____

7. A travelling salesman having merchandise samples or other merchandise for sale in his room

    A. keeps it there at his own risk
    B. can obtain limited coverage for loss by insuring it with the hotel or motel, which must provide such insurance or coverage at a fee
    C. may recover for any loss in any amount if the loss is due to the fault or negligence of the hotel or motel keeper
    D. will obtain coverage for loss by notifying the management in advance that he will have the property with him, and its value

7._____

8. Certain provisions of Section 201 apply to

    A. all parcel and check rooms
    B. parcel and check rooms in restaurants that do not charge a fee but do issue checks
    C. parcel and check rooms in hotels and motels, and restaurants in such hotels and motels
    D. only to parcel and check rooms that charge fees in hotels, motels and restaurants

8._____

9. The limit of liability for parcel and check rooms covered by this section is

    A. $75 if no excess valuation is declared and the loss is not due to negligence or fault on the part of the management
    B. $75 if no excess valuation is declared, but up to the lost property's full value if an excess valuation is declared and accepted by the management as evidenced by a written receipt
    C. $75 if no excess valuation is declared and $100 if an excess valuation is declared and the loss arises from the negligence or fault of the management
    D. $100 regardless of the circumstances of the loss

9._____

10. Generally, liability encompassed under Section 201 EXCLUDES losses

10._____

A. occasioned by fires not due to negligence
B. arising out of the management's negligence
C. for property not placed in a storage room, baggage room, parcel or check room, or in the hotel or motel safe
D. for stored property unless a check or receipt is given therefor

11. Assume that *P* has been injured as a result of the negligence of joint tort feasors *D* and *C*.
    As part of his action to recover damages, *P*

     11.____

    A. must join *D* and *C* as defendants
    B. has the right to name only *D* as a defendant
    C. has the right to name only *D* as a defendant, but only after he has settled with *C*
    D. is barred from any settlement before trial with either *D* or *C*

12. Assume that *A* was driving a car in a northerly direction and that *B* was driving a car along the same road in a southerly direction. *B*'s car crashed into *A*'s car solely as the result of a defective steering mechanism in *B*'s car, for which *B* could have brought a breach of warranty of merchantability action against the manufacturer of the car.
    What are *A*'s right under these circumstances?

     12.____

    A. *A*'s only remedy is against *B* in negligence.
    B. *A* has no cause of action in breach of warranty against the manufacturer of *B*'s car unless *A* and *B* are in privity with each other.
    C. *A*'s only remedy against the manufacturer of *B*'s car is in negligence.
    D. *A* has a cause of action in breach of warranty against the manufacturer of *B*'s car.

13. Assume that a mother negligently walks her 10-year-old child across the street against the light, and the child is injured while crossing by the negligent operation of *D*'s auto.
    It would be CORRECT to state that, in an action by the child against *D* for personal injuries,

     13.____

    A. the child of this age can not be guilty of negligence as a matter of law
    B. there is a rebuttable presumption that the child was also negligent
    C. the negligence of the mother is not imputed to the child
    D. the child in this case would have to prove that *D* was guilty of willful misconduct

14. Assume that *P*, while a patient in *X* Hospital, suffers personal injuries as the result of the medical malpractice of *D*, a staff physician of *X* Hospital.
    Under these circumstances, who is liable if *P* brings an action to recover for said injuries?

     14.____

    A. Only *D* is liable for negligence.
    B. *X* Hospital is liable for negligence.
    C. *X* Hospital is liable only for administrative negligence.
    D. *D* is liable only for willful negligence.

15. Assume that *F* negligently operates his auto so as to cause an accident with another car resulting in personal injuries to his son *P*, a passenger in *F*'s car.
    If *P*'s injuries exceed the no-fault threshold, *P*

     15.____

   A.   can recover for his personal injuries only against the driver of the other car involved in the accident

   B.   has no cause of action against *F*

   C.   has a cause of action against *F* only if he can prove willful misconduct on *F's* part

   D.   has a cause of action in negligence against *F* to recover for his personal injuries

16.   Assume that *D,* while carefully and without negligence, engaged in blasting on his premises, caused damage to P's adjacent building. The damage was solely the result of concussive force.
   What is *D's* liability under these circumstances?
   D is   16._____

   A.   liable to *P* under a strict liability rule without proof of fault

   B.   not liable to *P* unless *P* can prove negligence

   C.   liable to *P* only if rocks or debris thrown by *D's* blasting damaged *P's* property

   D.   not liable to *P*

17.   Assume that *D* has converted a rare book belonging to *A,* and is still in possession of the book after *A* has demanded its return.
   If *A* brings an action in conversion for damages, *A* is entitled to the   17._____

   A.   amount he paid for the book

   B.   market value of the book at the time of conversion

   C.   market value of the book at the time of judgment, if that is higher than the market value at the time of conversion

   D.   appraisal value of the book at the time of purchase

18.   *A* owed *C* $500. *B,* who told *A* he needed $500 for a few days, obtained that sum from *A* and promised to pay *C* the $500 the following week. *B* did not pay *C,* and *C* instituted an action against *B* for the money.
   Assuming that the necessary proof is preferred, what are the prospects for *C's* recovery in this case?   18._____

   A.   *C* cannot recover because there is no privity between *C* and *B.*

   B.   *C* may recover as a third party beneficiary of the contract between *A* and *B.*

   C.   *C* cannot recover because no consideration moved from *C* to *B.*

   D.   *C* may recover on the theory that *B* is a constructive trustee of the funds and the Court will impress such a trust to prevent unjust enrichment.

19.   *P* checked a parcel in a public check room at a railroad station and was given a stub with large red identifying numbers on it. In small print at the bottom of the check stub there was the legend: *This contract is made upon the following conditions: The charge is 50¢ a day or fraction thereof for each parcel checked. No claim shall be made in excess of $25.00 for loss or damage to any one parcel.* The parcel was lost through the negligence of the management. The parcel contained fur pieces valued at $5,000. *P* sues the check room operator for $5,000.
   In such a case, *P* may recover   19._____

   A.   only $25 because he is bound by the notice on the check stub on the limitation of liability

   B.   only $25 because by accepting the baggage check he accepted all the contractual provisions thereon

C. $5,000 because he did not have reasonable notice of the terms of the contract and, therefore, could not be deemed to have accepted them

D. $5,000 because no one who invites the public to do business may limit his liability where a loss occurs through negligence.

20. In charging a jury on the issue of damages where there has been a default by a builder in a construction contract which one of the following is NOT a correct charge?   20._____

    A. Where there is a substantial defect in the construction, generally the measure of damages is the cost of replacement or repair to conform to the contract.

    B. If the breach was unsubstantial and unintentional, the measure of damages is the contract price because the contract has not been performed.

    C. If replacement costs to correct the breach are major and are out of proportion to the good to be attained, the measure of damages is the difference in value between the building as contracted for and its value as built.

    D. Where a builder pleads substantial performance, the burden of proving the reason for the deviation from the contract and the proper deduction for such difference is on the builder.

———

KEY (CORRECT ANSWERS)

1.	C	6.	B	11.	B	16.	A
2.	B	7.	C	12.	D	17.	C
3.	A	8.	B	13.	C	18.	B
4.	D	9.	A	14.	B	19.	C
5.	D	10.	A	15.	D	20.	B

———

EXAMINATION SECTION
TEST 1

DIRECTIONS: Each question or incomplete statement is followed by several suggested answers or completions. Select the one that BEST answers the question or completes the statement. *PRINT THE LETTER OF THE CORRECT ANSWER IN THE SPACE AT THE RIGHT.*

1. *P* and *D* signed a contract for the proposed sale of Blackacre. The contract included a description of the property, the selling price, the amount of the purchase money mortgage, and the identity of the parties. It further provided that terms for the payment of principal and interest would be mutually agreed upon at the time the formal contract was concluded. Subsequently, *D* prepared a contract which provided a schedule of amortization which P found unsatisfactory. *P* prepared another contract with a somewhat different schedule which he signed and forwarded to *D*.
D refused to sign and refused to go forward with the sale. *P* brings an action in specific performance.
In such a case, specific performance should be

    A. *denied* because a material element of the contract is left for future negotiations
    B. *denied* because the terms of the mortgage payments had been omitted; the absence of any element in a contract for the sale of real property vitiates the contract under the Statute of Frauds
    C. *granted* because the defendant cannot take advantage of the failure of a condition precedent where he himself has prevented the condition from being met
    D. *granted* because the contract meets the requirements of the Statute of Frauds, the buyer and seller, the property and the price all being identified

1.____

2. Which one of the following statements concerning consideration as an element in contracts is NOT accurate?

    A. Consideration may be defined as a bargained-for exchange.
    B. A promise to make a gift is unenforceable.
    C. An exclusive dealing agreement is not without consideration because the party who gets the exclusive right makes no promise in return; the law implies a duty to use his best efforts.
    D. An agreement which permits one of the parties to terminate at will is enforceable against the other party who did not retain such a right.

2.____

3. *P* entered into a written contract with *D* which provided that if *P* could obtain a dealership for *D* from *X*, *P* would receive $10,000 and a percentage of the profits.
P did obtain the dealership for *D* by bribing *X*'s manager. *D* knew nothing of this. Subsequently, he does not pay *P*, and *P* brings an accounting action against *D*.
In such a case, *P*

    A. *can* recover because the contract is valid on its face and the illegal acts committed were not part of that agreement
    B. *cannot* recover because an agent may not recover from his principal compensation for obtaining a contract by illegal means not authorized by the principal
    C. *can* recover because *D* cannot assert as a defense a wrong committed against *X*
    D. *cannot* recover because of his illegal conduct but *D* cannot benefit thereby; *D* must hold the profits and the $10,000 as a constructive trustee for the benefit of *X*

3.____

4. *P*, who had a government contract for radar sets, entered into a contract with *D* for gears needed to construct the sets. Subsequently, *P* obtained an additional contract for such sets from the Government and advertised for bids for the gears he would need for the second contract. *D* notified *P* that unless he gave him the contract for the additional gears and agreed to pay him a higher price on all gears furnished, including the ones needed for the first contract, he would refuse to supply him with any gears at all. Because of the liquidated damage and default clauses in *P*'s contract with the Government and his inability to get enough gears to meet his commitments on the first contract if *D* breached, *P* agreed to *D*'s demands and entered into a new contract for all the gears at a higher price. Subsequently, *P* sued *D* to recover payments made for goods delivered
In such a case, *P*

4.＿＿＿

   A.   *should succeed* because the contract was voidable on the grounds of duress
   B.   *should lose* because, although he was subject to economic duress, the duress that avoids a contract is physical duress or fear of physical duress
   C.   *should lose* because there was a recission of the first contract and a valid new contract
   D.   *should succeed* partially because there was no consideration for the new price charged for the gears; *P* should recover the difference between the old contract price and the new contract price for the gears furnished for the first contract

5. Which one of the following is NOT a proper rule of damages for breach of a contract of sale of merchandise to be resold by a purchaser?

5.＿＿＿

   A.   The general rule is that the buyer who has contracted to resell goods to a customer is entitled to the difference between the market price on the date of the breach and the price he must pay for cover. In anticipatory breach, he may select either the contract date or the date he was notified that the seller would not perform.
   B.   If there are special circumstances made known to the seller at the time the contract was made that put him on notice that his failure to deliver would cause the buyer to breach a contract with his customer, and in fact that second contract is breached, the measure of damages is the damages paid by the buyer to his customer and expenses incurred to satisfy the buyer's breach to this customer.
   C.   If the breach is not substantial, the measure of damages is the difference between the value of full performance and the value of the performance that was proffered, or the cost of replacing the non-conforming goods, whichever is more; no buyer has a right to reject goods which substantially conform to the contract.
   D.   Mere knowledge by seller that buyer is purchasing for resale is not deemed notice of special circumstances that would entitle the buyer to recover consequential damages.

6. When researching a legal problem, the main objective is to locate primary (mandatory) authority within your jurisdiction.
Primary authority would NOT include

6.＿＿＿

   A.   legislation
   B.   judicial decisions
   C.   administrative rules
   D.   law revision commission reports

7. Assume that you are given the name of a case and the citation to either the official reports or unofficial reporter in which it is published.
The one of the following you should consult in order to obtain the parallel citation is

    A. the state Jurisprudence
    B. Shepard Case Citators
    C. the state Consolidated Laws Service
    D. Corpus Juris Secundum

8. Absent primary (mandatory) authority within this state relating to a legal question under consideration, you would consider persuasive (secondary) authority. Persuasive authority would NOT include

    A. other-state judicial decisions
    B. opinions of legal experts
    C. legislation of another state
    D. obiter dictum in reporter opinions

9. Where there has been no judicial interpretation relevant to a particular legal issue, what source other than the statute itself would you consult in order to determine the existence of documentation which might indicate the legislative intent of a statute enacted by the legislature of the state?

    A. American Jurisprudence 2nd
    B. Manual for the use of the Legislature of the State
    C. McKinney's Session Laws
    D. Abbott's Digest

10. Shepard Case Citators enable you to determine whether the cited case

    A. has been affirmed, reversed, or modified on appeal to a higher tribunal
    B. has been subsequently modified by a statute
    C. is discussed in Corpus Juris Secundum
    D. is listed in the Annotations in McKinney's Consolidated Laws

11. The Shepard Citator unit for Statutes does NOT permit you to shepardize

    A. opinions of the Attorney General of the United States
    B. United States Code
    C. United States treaties
    D. Unconsolidated Laws (McKinney)

12. Assume that you commence your research by using Abbott's Digest and find no cases under the Topic and Key Number assigned to your point of law.
In this situation, by using the same Topic and Key Number, you can extend your search to all of the following EXCEPT

    A. the Atlantic Digest
    B. the American Digest System
    C. Modern Federal Practice Digest
    D. American Law Reports 2d Digest

13. Rules promulgated by the Courts of the State are published in all of the following publications EXCEPT   13.____

    A. State Official Compilation of Codes, Rules, and Regulations
    B. Abbott's Digest
    C. New York Law Journal
    D. McKinney's Consolidated Laws

14. Which of the following is the official report in which cases decided by the New York Court of Appeals are published?   14.____

    A. Northeastern Reporter 2d
    B. New York Supplement 2d
    C. New York Reports 2d
    D. Miscellaneous Reports 2d

15. In tracing federal legislative history, all of the following should be considered in order to assist in determining the intent of Congress EXCEPT   15.____

    A. Congressional debates
    B. U.S. Government Manual, 1973-1974
    C. Congressional Committee published reports
    D. Congressional Committee published hearings

16. According to the Uniform System of Citations, 11th ed., which one of the following examples would be the proper method of citing the case of Courtney v. Kelmus, decided in the Supreme Court, State of New York, on December 1, 1944, and reported in volume 50 of the New York Supplement 2d on page 897 and in volume 182 of the Miscellaneous Reports on page 498?   16.____

    A. 182 Misc. 498, 50 N.Y.S.2d 897
    B. 50 N.Y.S.2d 897, 182 Misc. 498 (Sup. Ct. 1944)
    C. 182 Misc. 498 (Sup. Ct. 1944)
    D. 182 Misc. 498, 50 N.Y.S.2d 897 (Sup. Ct. 1944)

Questions 17-25.

DIRECTIONS: Questions 17 through 25 are to be answered SOLELY on the basis of case law and statutory law in the State.

17. What jurisdiction does the State acquire when a foreign corporation is *doing business* in this state?   17.____
The State

    A. acquires personal jurisdiction over the foreign corporation for any cause of action, no matter where the events which gave rise to it occurred
    B. acquires jurisdiction over only those acts committed by the foreign corporation in the State
    C. always acquires jurisdiction over all of the foreign corporation's foreign subsidiaries
    D. acquires no jurisdiction unless the foreign corporation's property can be attached

18. A defendant does NOT appear in an action when he   18.____

    A. makes a motion which has the effect of extending the time to answer
    B. serves a timely answer
    C. demands a complaint if one is not served with the summons in an action of the Supreme Court
    D. serves a timely notice of appearance

19. With respect to the granting of an order of attachment, it would be CORRECT to state   19.____
that such an order

    A. may be granted in a matrimonial action
    B. must be granted where defendant is not a resident or domiciliary of the state and plaintiff would be entitled to a money judgment
    C. is never granted against a New York domiciliary
    D. may be granted where defendant is not a resident or domiciliary of the state and plaintiff would be entitled to a money judgment

20. Which of the following is NOT the function of a bill of particulars?   20.____
To

    A. amplify the pleadings
    B. obtain your adversary's evidence
    C. limit proof at trial
    D. prevent surprise at trial

21. Which of the following statements concerning a motion for summary judgement is NOT   21.____
correct?

    A. Without a formal cross-motion, the court cannot grant summary judgment to a non-moving party.
    B. The motion shall be granted if the cause of action is established sufficiently to warrant the court as a matter of law in directing judgment.
    C. The motion shall be denied if there is a genuine factual issue requiring a trial.
    D. An affidavit by an attorney without personal knowledge of the facts is of no probative value.

22. Plaintiff may NOT conduct an examination before trial   22.____

    A. of a third-party defendant
    B. of a defendant unless plaintiff first obtains a court order
    C. of a non-party witness unless there are special circumstances shown
    D. unless a note of issue and statement of readiness have been filed

23. In a medical malpractice action based on defendant's alleged negligence in leaving a   23.____
surgical clamp inside plaintiff, the statute of limitations

    A. begins to run from the date of the operation
    B. may be extended by the court upon a showing of good cause
    C. need not be pleaded as an affirmative defense
    D. will not begin to run until plaintiff could reasonably have discovered the malpractice

24. When jurisdiction is acquired over a defendant solely on the basis of the *Long-arm* statute (CPLR 302), it would be CORRECT to state that   24.____

    A. New York has jurisdiction over every tortious act committed by the defendant outside New York causing injury to property within New York

    B. New York has jurisdiction over a cause of action against a New Jersey domiciliary who drives into New York and runs over plaintiff

    C. defendant's appearance in New York gives the court jurisdiction over causes of action not arising from acts enumerated in the statute

    D. defendant's ownership of real property in New York gives the court jurisdiction over every tortious act committed by him outside New York

25. Where plaintiff joins a claim that is not triable by jury with a claim that is triable by jury as of right, the plaintiff   25.____

    A. is entitled to a trial by jury on both claims of action

    B. has split his cause of action

    C. has waived his right to a jury trial on both claims where the claims are based on the same transactions and wrongs

    D. is entitled to a trial by jury only on the claim triable by jury as of right

―――――

KEY (CORRECT ANSWERS)

1.	A	11.	A
2.	D	12.	D
3.	B	13.	B
4.	A	14.	C
5.	C	15.	D
6.	D	16.	D
7.	B	17.	A
8.	C	18.	C
9.	C	19.	D
10.	A	20.	B

21.	A
22.	C
23.	D
24.	B
25.	C

―――――

40

EXAMINATION SECTION
TEST 1

DIRECTIONS: Each question or incomplete statement is followed by several suggested answers or completions. Select the one that BEST answers the question or completes the statement. *PRINT THE LETTER OF THE CORRECT ANSWER IN THE SPACE AT THE RIGHT.*

Questions 1-6.

DIRECTIONS: Questions 1 through 6 consist of descriptions of material to which a filing designation must be assigned.

Assume that the matters and cases described in the questions were referred for handling to a government legal office which has its files set up according to these file designations. The file designation consists of a number of characters and punctuation marks as described below.

The first character refers to agencies whose legal work is handled by this office. These agencies are numbered consecutively in the order in which they first submit a matter for attention, and are identified in an alphabetical card index. To date numbers have been assigned to agencies as follows:

Department of Correction	1
Police Department	2
Department of Traffic	3
Department of Consumer Affairs	4
Commission on Human Rights	5
Board of Elections	6
Department of Personnel	7
Board of Estimate	8

The second character is separated from the first character by a dash. The second character is the last digit of the year in which a particular lawsuit or matter is referred to the legal office.

The third character is separated from the second character by a colon and may consist of either of the following:

I. *A sub-number assigned to each lawsuit to which the agency is a party. Lawsuits are numbered consecutively regardless of year. (Lawsuits are brought by or against agency heads rather than agencies themselves, but references are made to agencies for the purpose of simplification.)*

or II. *A capital letter assigned to each matter other than a lawsuit according to subject, the subject being identified in an alphabetical index. To date, letters have been assigned to subjects as follows:*

Citizenship	A	Housing	E
Discrimination	B	Gambling	F
Residence Requirements	C	Freedom of Religion	G
Civil Service Examinations	D		

These referrals are numbered consecutively regardless of year. The first referral by a particular agency on citizenship, for example, would be designated A1, followed by A2, A3, etc.

If no reference is made in a question as to how many letters involving a certain subject or how many lawsuits have been referred by an agency, assume that it is the first.

For each question, choose the file designation which is MOST appropriate for filing the material described in the question.

1. In January 2010, two candidates in a 2009 civil service examination for positions with the Department of Correction filed a suit against the Department of Personnel seeking to set aside an educational requirement for the title.
   The Department of Personnel immediately referred the lawsuit to the legal office for handling.

   A. 1-9:1   B. 1-0:D1   C. 7-9:D1   D. 7-0:1

   1.____

2. In 2014, the Police Department made its sixth request for an opinion on whether an employee assignment proposed for 2015 could be considered discriminatory.

   A. 2-5:1-B6   B. 2-4:6   C. 2-4:1-B6   D. 2-4:B6

   2.____

3. In 2015, a lawsuit was brought by the Bay Island Action Committee against the Board of Estimate in which the plaintiff sought withdrawal of approval of housing for the elderly in the Bay Island area given by the Board in 2015.

   A. 8-3:1   B. 8-5:1   C. 8-3:B1   D. 8-5:E1

   3.____

4. In December 2014, community leaders asked the Police Department to ban outdoor meetings of a religious group on the grounds that the meetings were disrupting the area. Such meetings had been held from time to time during 2014. On January 31, 2015, the Police Department asked the government legal office for an opinion on whether granting this request would violate the worshippers' right to freedom of religion.

   A. 2-4:G-1   B. 2-5:G1   C. 2-5:B-1   D. 2-4:B1

   4.____

5. In 2014, a woman filed suit against the Board of Elections. She alleged that she had not been permitted to vote at her usual polling place in the 2013 election and had been told she was not registered there. She claimed that she had always voted there and that her record card had been lost. This was the fourth case of its type for this agency.

   A. 6-4:4   B. 6-3:C4   C. 3-4:6   D. 6-3:4

   5.____

6. A lawsuit was brought in 2011 by the Ace Pinball Machine Company against the Commissioner of Consumer Affairs. The lawsuit contested an ordinance which banned the use of pinball machines on the ground that they are gambling devices.
   This was the third lawsuit to which the Department of Consumer Affairs was a party.

   A. 4-1:1   B. 4-3:F1   C. 4-1:3   D. 3F-4:1

   6.____

7. You are instructed by your supervisor to type a statement that must be signed by the per-   7.____
son making the statement and by three witnesses to the signature. The typed statement
will take two pages and will leave no room for signatures if the normal margin is maintained at the bottom of the second page.
In this situation, the PREFERRED method is to type

    A. the signature lines below the normal margin on the second page
    B. nothing further and have the witnesses sign without a typed signature line
    C. the signature lines on a third page
    D. some of the text and the signature lines on a third page

8. Certain legal documents always begin with a statement of venue - that is, the county and   8.____
state in which the document is executed. This is usually boxed with a parentheses or
colons.
The one of the following documents that ALWAYS bears a statement of venue in a
prominent position at its head is a(n)

    A. affidavit   B. memorandum of law
    C. contract of sale   D. will

9. A court stenographer is to take stenographic notes and transcribe the statements of a   9.____
person under oath. The person has a heavy accent and speaks in ungrammatical and
broken English.
When he or she is transcribing the testimony, of the following, the BEST thing for them to
do is to

    A. transcribe the testimony exactly as spoken, making no grammatical changes
    B. make only the grammatical changes which would clarify the client's statements
    C. make all grammatical changes so that the testimony is in standard English form
    D. ask the client's permission before making any grammatical changes

10. When the material typed on a printed form does not fill the space provided, a Z-ruling is   10.____
frequently drawn to fill up the unused space.
The MAIN purpose of this practice is to

    A. make the document more pleasing to the eye
    B. indicate that the preceding material is correct
    C. insure that the document is not altered
    D. show that the lawyer has read it

11. After you had typed an original and five copies of a certain document, some changes   11.____
were made in ink on the original and were initialed by all the parties. The original was
signed by all the parties, and the signatures were notarized.
Which of the following should *generally* be typed on the copies BEFORE filing the original and the copies? The inked changes

    A. but not the signatures, initials, or notarial data
    B. the signatures and the initials but not the notarial data
    C. and the notarial data but not the signatures or initials
    D. the signatures, the initials, and the notarial data

12. The first paragraph of a noncourt agreement *generally* contains all of the following   12._____
EXCEPT the

   A. specific terms of the agreement
   B. date of the agreement
   C. purpose of the agreement
   D. names of the parties involved

13. When typing an answer in a court proceeding, the place where the word ANSWER   13._____
should be typed on the first page of the document is

   A. at the upper left-hand corner
   B. below the index number and to the right of the box containing the names of the parties to the action
   C. above the index number and to the right of the box containing the names of the parties to the action
   D. to the left of the names of the attorneys for the defendant

14. Which one of the following statements BEST describes the legal document called an   14._____
acknowledgment?
It is

   A. an answer to an affidavit
   B. a receipt issued by the court when a document is filed
   C. proof of service of a summons
   D. a declaration that a signature is valid

15. Suppose you typed the original and three copies of a legal document which was   15._____
dictated by an attorney in your office. He has already signed the original copy, and corrections have been made on all copies.
Regarding the copies, which one of the following procedures is the PROPER
one to follow?

   A. Leave the signature line blank on the copies
   B. Ask the attorney to sign the copies
   C. Print or type the attorney's name on the signature line on the copies
   D. Sign your name to the copies followed by the attorney's initials

16. Suppose your office is defending a particular person in a court action. This person   16._____
comes to the office and asks to see some of the lawyer's working papers in his file. The
lawyer assigned to the case is out of the office at the time.
You SHOULD

   A. permit him to examine his entire file as long as he does not remove any materials from it
   B. make an appointment for the caller to come back later when the lawyer will be there
   C. ask him what working papers he wants to see and show him only those papers
   D. tell him that he needs written permission from the lawyer in order to see any records

17. Suppose that you receive a phone call from an official who is annoyed about a letter from   17._____
your office which she just received. The lawyer who dictated the letter is not in the office
at the moment.
Of the following, the BEST action for you to take is to

    A.   explain that the lawyer is out but that you will ask the lawyer to return her call when
he returns
    B.   take down all of the details of her complaint and tell her that you will get back to her
with an explanation
    C.   refer to the proper file so that you can give her an explanation of the reasons for the
letter over the phone
    D.   make an appointment for her to stop by the office to speak with the lawyer

18. Suppose that you have taken dictation for an interoffice memorandum. You are asked to   18._____
prepare it for distribution to four lawyers in your department whose names are given to
you. You will type an original and make four copies. Which one of the following is COR-
RECT with regard to the typing of the lawyers' names?
The names of all of the lawyers should appear

    A.   *only* on the original
    B.   on the original and each copy should have the name of one lawyer
    C.   on each of the copies but not on the original
    D.   on the original and on all of the copies

19. Regarding the correct typing of punctuation, the GENERALLY accepted practice is that   19._____
there should be

    A.   two spaces after a semi-colon
    B.   one space before an apostrophe used in the body of a word
    C.   no space between parentheses and the matter enclosed
    D.   one space before and after a hyphen

20. Suppose you have just completed typing an original and two copies of a letter   20._____
requesting information. The original is to be signed by a lawyer in your office. The first
copy is for the files, and the second is to be used as a reminder to follow up.
The PROPER time to file the file copy of the letter is

    A.   after the letter has been signed and corrections have been made on the copies
    B.   before you take the letter to the lawyer for his signature
    C.   after a follow-up letter has been sent
    D.   after a response to the letter has been received

21. A secretary in a legal office has just typed a letter. She has typed the copy distribution   21._____
notation on the copies to indicate *blind copy distribution*. This *blind copy* notation shows
that

    A.   copies of the letter are being sent to persons that the addressee does not know
    B.   copies of the letter are being sent to other persons without the addressee's knowledge
    C.   a copy of the letter will be enlarged for a legally blind person
    D.   a copy of the letter is being given as an extra copy to the addressee

22. Suppose that one of the attorneys in your office dictates material to you without indicating punctuation. He has asked that you give him, as soon as possible, a single copy of a rough draft to be triple-spaced so that he can make corrections.
Of the following, what is the BEST thing for you to do in this situation?

   22.____

   A. Assume that no punctuation is desired in the material
   B. Insert the punctuation as you type the rough draft
   C. Transcribe the material exactly as dictated, but attach a note to the attorney stating your suggested changes
   D. Before you start to type the draft, tell the attorney you want to read back your notes so that he can indicate punctuation

23. When it is necessary to type a mailing notation such as CERTIFIED, REGISTERED, or FEDEX on an envelope, the GENERALLY accepted place to type it is

   23.____

   A. directly above the address
   B. in the area below where the stamp will be affixed
   C. in the lower left-hand corner
   D. in the upper left-hand corner

24. When taking a citation of a case in shorthand, which of the following should you write FIRST if you are having difficulty keeping up with the dictation?

   24.____

   A. Volume and page number   B. Title of volume
   C. Name of plaintiff   D. Name of defendant

25. All of the following abbreviations and their meanings are correctly paired EXCEPT

   25.____

   A. viz. - namely   B. ibid. - refer
   C. n.b. - note well   D. q.v. - which see

KEY (CORRECT ANSWERS)

1.	D		11.	D
2.	D		12.	A
3.	B		13.	B
4.	B		14.	D
5.	A		15.	C
6.	C		16.	B
7.	D		17.	A
8.	A		18.	D
9.	A		19.	C
10.	C		20.	A

21.	B
22.	B
23.	B
24.	A
25.	B

EXAMINATION SECTION
TEST 1

DIRECTIONS: Each question or incomplete statement is followed by several suggested answers or completions. Select the one that BEST answers the question or completes the statement. *PRINT THE LETTER OF THE CORRECT ANSWER IN THE SPACE AT THE RIGHT.*

Questions 1-9.

DIRECTIONS: Questions 1 through 9 consist of sentences which may or may not be examples of good English usage. Consider grammar, punctuation, spelling, capitalization, awkwardness, etc. Examine each sentence, and then choose the correct statement about it from the four choices below it. If the English usage in the sentence given is better than it would be with any of the changes suggested in options B, C, and D, choose option A. Do not choose an option that will change the meaning of the sentence.

1. According to Judge Frank, the grocer's sons found guilty of assault and sentenced last Thursday.   1.____

    A. This is an example of acceptable writing.
    B. A comma should be placed after the word *sentenced*.
    C. The word *were* should be placed after *sons*
    D. The apostrophe in *grocer's* should be placed after the *s*.

2. The department heads assistant said that the stenographers should type duplicate copies of all contracts, leases, and bills.   2.____

    A. This is an example of acceptable writing.
    B. A comma should be placed before the word *contracts*.
    C. An apostrophe should be placed before the *s* in *heads*.
    D. Quotation marks should be placed before *the stenographers* and after *bills*.

3. The lawyers questioned the men to determine who was the true property owner?   3.____

    A. This is an example of acceptable writing.
    B. The phrase *questioned the men* should be changed to *asked the men questions*.
    C. The word *was* should be changed to *were*.
    D. The question mark should be changed to a period.

4. The terms stated in the present contract are more specific than those stated in the previous contract.   4.____

    A. This is an example of acceptable writing.
    B. The word *are* should be changed to *is*.
    C. The word *than* should be changed to *then*.
    D. The word *specific* should be changed to *specified*.

5. Of the lawyers considered, the one who argued more skillful was chosen for the job.   5.____

    A. This is an example of acceptable writing.
    B. The word *more* should be replaced by the word *most*.
    C. The word *skillful* should be replaced by the word *skillfully,*
    D. The word *chosen* should be replaced by the word *selected*.

6. Each of the states has a court of appeals; some states have circuit courts.   6._____

    A.   This is an example of acceptable writing.
    B.   The semi-colon should be changed to a comma.
    C.   The word *has* should be changed to *have*.
    D.   The word *some* should be capitalized.

7. The court trial has greatly effected the child's mental condition.   7._____

    A.   This is an example of acceptable writing.
    B.   The word *effected* should be changed to *affected*.
    C.   The word *greatly* should be placed after *effected*.
    D.   The apostrophe in *child's* should be placed after the *s*.

8. Last week, the petition signed by all the officers was sent to the Better Business Bureau.   8._____

    A.   This is an example of acceptable writing.
    B.   The phrase *last week* should be placed after *officers*.
    C.   A comma should be placed after *petition*.
    D.   The word *was* should be changed to *were*.

9. Mr. Farrell claims that he requested form A-12, and three booklets describing court procedures.   9._____

    A.   This is an example of acceptable writing.
    B.   The word *that* should be eliminated.
    C.   A colon should be placed after *requested*.
    D.   The comma after *A-12* should be eliminated.

Questions 10-21.

DIRECTIONS: Questions 10 through 21 contain a word in capital letters followed by four suggested meanings of the word. For each question, choose the BEST meaning for the word in capital letters.

10. SIGNATORY - A   10._____

    A.   lawyer who draws up a legal document
    B.   document that must be signed by a judge
    C.   person who signs a document
    D.   true copy of a signature

11. RETAINER - A   11._____

    A.   fee paid to a lawyer for his services
    B.   document held by a third party
    C.   court decision to send a prisoner back to custody pending trial
    D.   legal requirement to keep certain types of files

12. BEQUEATH - To   12._____

    A.   receive assistance from a charitable organization
    B.   give personal property by will to another
    C.   transfer real property from one person to another
    D.   receive an inheritance upon the death of a relative

13. RATIFY - To   13.____

    A. approve and sanction   B. forego
    C. produce evidence   D. summarize

14. CODICIL - A   14.____

    A. document introduced in evidence in a civil action
    B. subsection of a law
    C. type of legal action that can be brought by a plaintiff
    D. supplement or an addition to a will

15. ALIAS   15.____

    A. Assumed name   B. In favor of
    C. Against   D. A writ

16. PROXY - A(n)   16.____

    A. phony document in a real estate transaction
    B. opinion by a judge of a civil court
    C. document containing appointment of an agent
    D. summons in a lawsuit

17. ALLEGED   17.____

    A. Innocent   B. Asserted
    C. Guilty   D. Called upon

18. EXECUTE - To   18.____

    A. complete a legal document by signing it
    B. set requirements
    C. render services to a duly elected executive of a municipality
    D. initiate legal action such as a lawsuit

19. NOTARY PUBLIC - A   19.____

    A. lawyer who is running for public office
    B. judge who hears minor cases
    C. public officer, one of whose functions is to administer oaths
    D. lawyer who gives free legal services to persons unable to pay

20. WAIVE - To   20.____

    A. disturb a calm state of affairs
    B. knowingly renounce a right or claim
    C. pardon someone for a minor fault
    D. purposely mislead a person during an investigation

21. ARRAIGN - To   21.____

    A. prevent an escape   B. defend a prisoner
    C. verify a document   D. accuse in a court of law

Questions 22-40.

DIRECTIONS: Questions 22 through 40 each consist of four words which may or may not be spelled correctly. If you find an error in
only one word, mark your answer A;
any two words, mark your answer B;
any three words, mark your answer C;
none of these words, mark your answer D.

22.	occurrence	Febuary	privilege	similiar	22.____
23.	separate	transferring	analyze	column	23.____
24.	develop	license	bankrupcy	abreviate	24.____
25.	subpoena	arguement	dissolution	foreclosure	25.____
26.	exaggerate	fundamental	significance	warrant	26.____
27.	citizen	endorsed	marraige	appraissal	27.____
28.	precedant	univercity	observence	preliminary	28.____
29.	stipulate	negligence	judgment	prominent	29.____
30.	judisial	whereas	release	guardian	30.____
31.	appeal	larcenny	transcrip	jurist	31.____
32.	petition	tenancy	agenda	insurance	32.____
33.	superfical	premise	morgaged	maintainance	33.____
34.	testamony	publically	installment	possessed	34.____
35.	escrow	decree	eviction	miscelaneous	35.____
36.	securitys	abeyance	adhere	corporate	36.____
37.	kaleidoscope	anesthesia	vermilion	tafetta	37.____
38.	congruant	barrenness	plebescite	vigilance	38.____
39.	picnicing	promisory	resevoir	omission	39.____
40.	supersede	banister	wholly	seize	40.____

KEY (CORRECT ANSWERS)

1.	C	11.	A	21.	D	31.	B
2.	C	12.	B	22.	B	32.	D
3.	D	13.	A	23.	D	33.	C
4.	A	14.	D	24.	B	34.	B
5.	C	15.	A	25.	A	35.	A
6.	A	16.	C	26.	D	36.	A
7.	B	17.	B	27.	B	37.	A
8.	A	18.	A	28.	C	38.	B
9.	D	19.	C	29.	D	39.	C
10.	C	20.	B	30.	A	40.	D

EXAMINATION SECTION
TEST 1

DIRECTIONS: Each question or incomplete statement is followed by several suggested answers or completions. Select the one that BEST answers the question or completes the statement. *PRINT THE LETTER OF THE CORRECT ANSWER IN THE SPACE AT THE RIGHT.*

Questions 1-50.

DIRECTIONS: Each of Questions 1 through 50 consists of a word in capital letters followed by four suggested meanings of the word. For each question, choose the word or phrase which means MOST NEARLY the same as the word in capital letters.

1. ABUT   1.____
    A. abandon   B. assist   C. border on   D. renounce

2. ABSCOND   2.____
    A. draw in   B. give up
    C. refrain from   D. deal off

3. BEQUEATH   3.____
    A. deaden   B. hand down   C. make sad   D. scold

4. BOGUS   4.____
    A. sad   B. false   C. shocking   D. stolen

5. CALAMITY   5.____
    A. disaster   B. female   C. insanity   D. patriot

6. COMPULSORY   6.____
    A. binding   B. ordinary   C. protected   D. ruling

7. CONSIGN   7.____
    A. agree with   B. benefit
    C. commit   D. drive down

8. DEBILITY   8.____
    A. failure   B. legality
    C. quality   D. weakness

9. DEFRAUD   9.____
    A. cheat   B. deny
    C. reveal   D. tie

10. DEPOSITION   10.____
    A. absence   B. publication
    C. removal   D. testimony

11. DOMICILE   11.____
    A. anger   B. dwelling
    C. tame   D. willing

53

12. **HEARSAY**
    A. selfish   B. serious   C. rumor   D. unlikely

    12.___

13. **HOMOGENEOUS**
    A. human   B. racial   C. similar   D. unwise

    13.___

14. **ILLICIT**
    A. understood   B. uneven   C. unkind   D. unlawful

    14.___

15. **LEDGER**
    A. book of accounts   B. editor
    C. periodical   D. shelf

    15.___

16. **NARRATIVE**
    A. gossip   B. natural   C. negative   D. story

    16.___

17. **PLAUSIBLE**
    A. reasonable   B. respectful   C. responsible   D. rightful

    17.___

18. **RECIPIENT**
    A. absentee   B. receiver   C. speaker   D. substitute

    18.___

19. **SUBSTANTIATE**
    A. appear for   B. arrange
    C. confirm   D. combine

    19.___

20. **SURMISE**
    A. aim   B. break   C. guess   D. order

    20.___

21. **ALTER EGO**
    A. business partner   B. confidential friend
    C. guide   D. subconscious conflict

    21.___

22. **FOURTH ESTATE**
    A. the aristocracy   B. the clergy
    C. the judiciary   D. the newspapers

    22.___

23. **IMPEACH**
    A. accuse   B. find guilty
    C. remove   D. try

    23.___

24. **PROPENSITY**
    A. dislike   B. helpfulness
    C. inclination   D. supervision

    24.___

25. **SPLENETIC**
    A. charming   B. peevish   C. shining   D. sluggish

    25.___

26. **SUBORN**
    A. bribe someone to commit perjury
    B. demote someone several levels in rank
    C. deride
    D. substitute

    26.___

27. TALISMAN
    A. charm
    C. prayer shawl
    B. juror
    D. native

27.___

28. VITREOUS
    A. corroding
    C. nourishing
    B. glassy
    D. sticky

28.___

29. WRY
    A. comic   B. grained   C. resilient   D. twisted

29.___

30. SIGNATORY
    A. lawyer who draws up a legal document
    B. document that must be signed by a judge
    C. person who signs a document
    D. true copy of a signature

30.___

31. RETAINER
    A. fee paid to a lawyer for his services
    B. document held by a third party
    C. court decision to send a prisoner back to custody pending trial
    D. legal requirement to keep certain types of files

31.___

32. BEQUEATH
    A. to receive assistance from a charitable organization
    B. to give personal property by will to another
    C. to transfer real property from one person to another
    D. to receive an inheritance upon the death of a relative

32.___

33. RATIFY
    A. approve and sanction
    C. produce evidence
    B. forego
    D. summarize

33.___

34. CODICIL
    A. document introduced in evidence in a civil action
    B. subsection of a law
    C. type of legal action that can be brought by a plaintiff
    D. supplement or an addition to a will

34.___

35. ALIAS
    A. assumed name   B. in favor of   C. against   D. a writ

35.___

36. PROXY
    A. a phony document in a real estate transaction
    B. an opinion by a judge of a civil court
    C. a document containing appointment of an agent
    D. a summons in a lawsuit

36.___

37. ALLEGED
    A. innocent   B. asserted   C. guilty   D. called upon

37.___

38. EXECUTE
    A. to complete a legal document by signing it
    B. to set requirements
    C. to render services to a duly elected executive of a municipality
    D. to initiate legal action such as a lawsuit

38.____

39. NOTARY PUBLIC
    A. lawyer who is running for public office
    B. judge who hears minor cases
    C. public officer, one of whose functions is to administer oaths
    D. lawyer who gives free legal services to persons unable to pay

39.____

40. WAIVE
    A. to disturb a calm state of affairs
    B. to knowingly renounce a right or claim
    C. to pardon someone for a minor fault
    D. to purposely mislead a person during an investigation

40.____

41. ARRAIGN
    A. to prevent an escape
    B. to defend a prisoner
    C. to verify a document
    D. to accuse in a court of law

41.____

42. VOLUNTARY
    A. by free choice   B. necessary
    C. important   D. by design

42.____

43. INJUNCTION
    A. act of prohibiting   B. process of inserting
    C. means of arbitrating   D. freedom of action

43.____

44. AMICABLE
    A. compelled   B. friendly
    C. unimportant   D. insignificant

44.____

45. CLOSED SHOP
    A. one that employs only members of a union
    B. one that employs union members and unaffiliated employees
    C. one that employs only employees with previous experience
    D. one that employs skilled and unskilled workers

45.____

46. ABDUCT
    A. lead   B. kidnap   C. sudden   D. worthless

46.____

47. BIAS
    A. ability   B. envy   C. prejudice   D. privilege

47.____

48. COERCE
    A. cancel   B. force   C. rescind   D. rugged

48.____

49. CONDONE   49.___
    A. combine   B. pardon   C. revive   D. spice

50. CONSISTENCY   50.___
    A. bravery   B. readiness
    C. strain   D. uniformity

KEY (CORRECT ANSWERS)

1. C	11. B	21. B	31. A	41. D
2. D	12. C	22. D	32. B	42. A
3. B	13. C	23. A	33. A	43. A
4. B	14. D	24. C	34. D	44. B
5. A	15. A	25. B	35. A	45. A
6. A	16. D	26. A	36. C	46. B
7. C	17. A	27. A	37. B	47. C
8. D	18. B	28. B	38. A	48. B
9. A	19. C	29. D	39. C	49. B
10. D	20. C	30. C	40. B	50. D

TEST 2

DIRECTIONS: Each question or incomplete statement is followed by several suggested answers or completions. Select the one that BEST answers the question or completes the statement. *PRINT THE LETTER OF THE CORRECT ANSWER IN THE SPACE AT THE RIGHT.*

1. In the sentence, *The prisoner was fractious when brought to the station house*, the word *fractious* means MOST NEARLY

   A. penitent   B. talkative
   C. irascible   D. broken-hearted

   1.____

2. In the sentence, *The judge was implacable when the attorney pleaded for leniency*, the word *implacable* means MOST NEARLY

   A. inexorable   B. disinterested
   C. inattentive   D. indifferent

   2.____

3. In the sentence, *The court ordered the mendacious statements stricken from the record*, the word *mendacious* means MOST NEARLY

   A. begging   B. lying
   C. threatening   D. lengthy

   3.____

4. In the sentence, *The district attorney spoke in a strident voice*, the word *strident* means MOST NEARLY

   A. loud   B. harsh-sounding
   C. sing-song   D. low

   4.____

5. In the sentence, *The speaker had a predilection for long sentences*, the word *predilection* means MOST NEARLY

   A. aversion   B. talent
   C. propensity   D. diffidence

   5.____

6. A person who has an uncontrollable desire to steal without need is called a

   A. dipsomaniac   B. kleptomaniac
   C. monomaniac   D. pyromaniac

   6.____

7. In the sentence, *Malice was immanent in all his remarks*, the word *immanent* means MOST NEARLY

   A. elevated   B. inherent
   C. threatening   D. foreign

   7.____

8. In the sentence, *The extant copies of the document were found in the safe*, the word *extant* means MOST NEARLY

   A. existing   B. original
   C. forged   D. duplicate

   8.____

9. In the sentence, *The recruit was more complaisant after the captain spoke to him*, the word *complaisant* means MOST NEARLY

   A. calm   B. affable
   C. irritable   D. confident

   9.____

10. In the sentence, *The man was captured under highly creditable circumstances*, the word *creditable* means MOST NEARLY
    A. doubtful   B. believable
    C. praiseworthy   D. unexpected
10.____

11. In the sentence, *His superior officers were more sagacious than he*, the word *sagacious* means MOST NEARLY
    A. shrewd   B. obtuse
    C. absurd   D. verbose
11.____

12. In the sentence, *He spoke with impunity*, the word *impunity* means MOST NEARLY
    A. rashness   B. caution
    C. without fear   D. immunity
12.____

13. In the sentence, *The new officer displayed unusual temerity during the emergency*, the word *temerity* means MOST NEARLY
    A. fear   B. rashness
    C. calmness   D. anxiety
13.____

14. In the sentence, *The portions of food were parsimoniously served*, the word *parsimoniously* means MOST NEARLY
    A. stingily   B. piously
    C. elaborately   D. generously
14.____

15. In the sentence, *Generally the speaker's remarks were sententious*, the word *sententious* means MOST NEARLY
    A. verbose   B. witty
    C. argumentative   D. pithy
15.____

Questions 16-20.

DIRECTIONS: Next to the number which corresponds with the number of each item in Column I, place the letter preceding the adjective in Column II which BEST describes the persons in Column I.

COLUMN I		COLUMN II	
16.	Talkative woman	A.	abstemious
17.	Person on a reducing diet	B.	pompous
18.	Scholarly professor	C.	erudite
19.	Man who seldom speaks	D.	benevolent
20.	Charitable person	E.	docile
		F.	loquacious
		G.	indefatigable
		H.	taciturn

16.____
17.____
18.____
19.____
20.____

Questions 21-25.

DIRECTIONS:　Next to the number which corresponds with the number preceding each profession in Column I, place the letter preceding the word in Column II which BEST explains the subject matter of that profession.

COLUMN I		COLUMN II	
21.	Geologist	A. animals	21.___
22.	Oculist	B. eyes	22.___
23.	Podiatrist	C. feet	23.___
24.	Palmist	D. fortune-telling	24.___
25.	Zoologist	E. language	25.___
		F. rocks	
		G. stamps	
		H. woman	

Questions 26-30.

DIRECTIONS:　Next to the number corresponding to the number of each of the words in Column I, place the letter preceding the word in Column II that is MOST NEARLY OPPOSITE to it in meaning.

COLUMN I		COLUMN II	
26.	comely	A. beautiful	26.___
27.	eminent	B. cowardly	27.___
28.	frugal	C. kind	28.___
29.	gullible	D. sedate	29.___
30.	valiant	E. shrewd	30.___
		F. ugly	
		G. unknown	
		H. wasteful	

KEY (CORRECT ANSWERS)

1.	C	11.	A	21.	F
2.	A	12.	D	22.	B
3.	B	13.	B	23.	C
4.	B	14.	A	24.	D
5.	C	15.	D	25.	A
6.	B	16.	F	26.	F
7.	B	17.	A	27.	G
8.	A	18.	C	28.	H
9.	B	19.	H	29.	E
10.	C	20.	D	30.	B

INTERVIEWING

EXAMINATION SECTION
TEST 1

DIRECTIONS : Each question or incomplete statement is followed by several suggested answers or completions. Select the one that BEST answers the question or completes the statement. *PRINT THE LETTER OF THE CORRECT ANSWER IN THE SPACE AT THE RIGHT.*

1. Of the following, the MAIN advantage to the supervisor of using the indirect (or nondirective) interview, in which he asks only guiding questions and encourages the employee to do most of the talking, is that he can   1._____

    A. obtain a mass of information about the employee in a very short period of time
    B. easily get at facts which the employee wishes to conceal
    C. get answers which are not slanted or biased in order to win his favor
    D. effectively deal with an employee's serious emotional problems

2. An interviewer under your supervision routinely closes his interview with a reassuring remark such as, "I'm sure you soon will be well," or "Everything will soon be all right." This practice is USUALLY considered   2._____

    A. *advisable,* chiefly because the interviewer may make the patient feel better
    B. *inadvisable,* chiefly because it may cause a patient who is seriously ill to doubt the worker's understanding of the situation
    C. *advisable,* chiefly because the patient becomes more receptive if further interviews are needed
    D. *inadvisable,* chiefly because the interviewer should usually not show that he is emotionally involved

3. An interviewer has just ushered out a client he has interviewed. As the interviewer is preparing to leave, the client mentions a fact that seems to contradict the information he has given.
Of the following, it would be BEST for the interviewer at this time to   3._____

    A. make no response but write the fact down in his report and plan to come back another day
    B. point out to the client that he has contradicted himself and ask for an explanation
    C. ask the client to elaborate on the comment and attempt to find out further information about the fact
    D. disregard the comment since the client was probably exhausted and not thinking clearly

4. A client who is being interviewed insists on certain facts. The interviewer knows that these statements are incorrect. In regard to the rest of the client's statements, the interviewer is MOST justified to   4._____

    A. disregard any information the client gives which cannot be verified
    B. try to discover other misstatements by confronting the client with the discrepancy
    C. consider everything else which the client has said as the truth unless proved otherwise
    D. ask the client to prove his statements

5. Immediately after the interviewer identifies himself to a client, she says in a hysterical voice that he is not to be trusted.
   Of the following, the BEST course of action for the interviewer to follow would be to

   A. tell the woman sternly that if she does not stay calm, he will leave
   B. assure the woman that there is no cause to worry
   C. ignore the woman until she becomes quiet
   D. ask the woman to explain her problem

   5.____

6. Assume that you are an interviewer and that one of your interviewees has asked you for advice on dealing with a personal problem.
   Of the following, the BEST action for you to take is to

   A. tell him about a similar problem which you know worked out well
   B. advise him not to worry
   C. explain that the problem is quite a usual one and that the situation will be brighter soon
   D. give no opinion and change the subject when practicable

   6.____

7. All of the following are, *generally,* good approaches for an interviewer to use in order to improve his interviews EXCEPT

   A. developing a routine approach so that interviews can be standardized
   B. comparing his procedure with that of others engaged in similar work
   C. reviewing each interview critically, picking out one or two weak points to concentrate on improving
   D. comparing his own more successful and less successful interviews

   7.____

8. Assume that a supervisor suggests at a staff meeting that digital recorders be provided for interviewers. Following are four arguments *against* the use of digital recorders that are raised by other members of the staff that might be valid:
   I.   Recorded interviews provide too much unnecessary information
   II. Recorded interviews provide no record of manner or gestures.
   III. Digital recorders are too cumbersome and difficult for the average supervisor to manage.
   IV. Digital recorders may inhibit the interviewee.
   Which one of the following choices MOST accurately classifies the above into those which are generally *valid* and those which are *not*?

   A. I and II are generally valid, but III and IV are not.
   B. IV is generally valid, but I, II and III are not.
   C. I, II and IV are generally valid, but III is not.
   D. I, II, III and IV are generally valid.

   8.____

9. During an interview the PRIMARY advantage of the technique of using questions as opposed to allowing the interviewee to talk freely is that questioning

   A. gives the interviewer greater control
   B. provides a more complete picture
   C. makes the interviewee more relaxed
   D. decreases the opportunity for exaggeration

   9.____

10. Assume that, in conducting an interview, an interviewer takes into consideration the age, sex, education, and background of the subject.
This practice is GENERALLY considered

    A. *undesirable,* mainly because an interviewer may be prejudiced by such factors
    B. *desirable,* mainly because these are factors which might influence a person's response to certain questions
    C. *undesirable,* mainly because these factors rarely have any bearing on the matter being investigated
    D. *desirable,* mainly because certain categories of people answer certain questions in the same way

10.____

11. If a client should begin to tell his life story during an interview, the BEST course of action for an interviewer to take is to

    A. interrupt immediately and insist that they return to business
    B. listen attentively until the client finishes and then ask if they can return to the subject
    C. pretend to have other business and come back later to see the client
    D. interrupt politely at an appropriate point and direct the client's attention to the subject

11.____

12. An interviewer who is trying to discover the circumstances surrounding a client's accident would be MOST successful during an interview if he avoided questions which

    A. lead the client to discuss the matter in detail
    B. can easily be answered by either "yes" or "no"
    C. ask for specific information
    D. may be embarrassing or annoying to the client

12.____

13. A client being interviewed may develop an emotional reaction (positive or negative) toward the interviewer. The BEST attitude for the interviewer to take toward such feelings is that they are

    A. *inevitable;* they should be accepted but kept under control
    B. *unusual;* they should be treated impersonally
    C. *obstructive;* they should be resisted at all costs
    D. *abnormal;* they should be eliminated as soon as possible

13.____

14. Encouraging the client being interviewed to talk freely at first is a technique that is supported by all of the following reasons EXCEPT that it

    A. tends to counteract any preconceived ideas that the interviewer may have entertained about the client
    B. gives the interviewer a chance to learn the best method of approach to obtain additional information
    C. inhibits the client from looking to the interviewer for support and advice
    D. allows the client to reveal the answers to many questions before they are asked

14.____

15. Of the following, *generally,* the MOST effective way for an interviewer to assure full cooperation from the client he is interviewing is to

    A. sympathize with the client's problems and assure him of concern
    B. tell a few jokes before beginning to ask questions

15.____

C. convince the patient that the answers to the questions will help him as well as the interviewer

D. arrange the interview when the client feels best

16. Since many elderly people are bewildered and helpless when interviewed, special consideration should be given to them.
Of the following, the BEST way for an interviewer to *initially* approach elderly clients who express anxiety and fear is to

    16.____

A. assure them that they have nothing to worry about
B. listen patiently and show interest in them
C. point out the specific course of action that is best for them
D. explain to them that many people have overcome much greater difficulties

17. Assume that, in planning an initial interview, an interviewer determines in advance what information is needed in order to fulfill the purpose of the interview.
Of the following, this procedure usually does NOT

    17.____

A. reduce the number of additional interviews required
B. expedite the processing of the case
C. improve public opinion of the interviewer's agency
D. assure the cooperation of the person interviewed

    17.____

18. Sometimes an interviewer deliberately introduces his own personal interests and opinions into an interview with a client.
In general, this practice should be considered

    18.____

A. *desirable,* primarily because the relationship between client and interviewer becomes social rather than businesslike
B. *undesirable,* primarily because the client might complain to his supervisor
C. *desirable;* primarily because the focus of attention is directed toward the client
D. *undesirable;* primarily because an argument between client and interviewer could result

19. The one of the following types of interviewees who presents the LEAST difficult problem to handle is the person who

    19.____

A. answers with a great many qualifications
B. talks at length about unrelated subjects so that the interviewer cannot ask questions
C. has difficulty understanding the interviewer's vocabulary
D. breaks into the middle of sentences and completes them with a meaning of his own

20. A man being interviewed is entitled to Medicaid, but he refuses to sign up for it because he says he cannot accept any form of welfare.
Of the following, the *best* course of action for an interviewer to take FIRST is to

    20.____

A. try to discover the reason for his feeling this way
B. tell him that he should be glad financial help is available
C. explain that others cannot help him if he will not help himself
D. suggest that he speak to someone who is already on Medicaid

21. Of the following, the outcome of an interview by an interviewer depends MOST heavily on the

    A. personality of the interviewee
    B. personality of the interviewer
    C. subject matter of the questions asked
    D. interaction between interviewer and interviewee

21.____

22. Some clients being interviewed by an interviewer are primarily interested in making a favorable impression. The interviewer should be aware of the fact that such clients are MORE likely than *other* clients to

    A. try to anticipate the answers the interviewer is looking for
    B. answer all questions openly and frankly
    C. try to assume the role of interviewer
    D. be anxious to get the interview over as quickly as possible

22.____

23. The type of interview which a hospital care interviewer usually conducts is *substantially different* from most interviewing situations in all of the following aspects EXCEPT the

    A. setting
    C. techniques employed
    B. kinds of clients
    D. kinds of problems

23.____

24. During an interview, an interviewer uses a "leading question."
This type of question is so-called because it, *generally.,*

    A. starts a series of questions about one topic
    B. suggests the answer which the interviewer wants
    C. forms the basis for a following "trick" question
    D. sets, at the beginning, the tone of the interview

24.____

25. An interviewer may face various difficulties when he tries to obtain information from a client.
Of the following, the difficulty which is EASIEST for the interviewer to *overcome* occurs when a client

    A. is unwilling to reveal the information
    B. misunderstands what information is needed
    C. does not have the information available to him
    D. is unable to coherently give the information requested

25.____

KEY (CORRECT ANSWERS)

1.	C		11.	D
2.	B		12.	B
3.	C		13.	A
4.	C		14.	C
5.	D		15.	C
6.	D		16.	B
7.	A		17.	D
8.	C		18.	D
9.	A		19.	C
10.	B		20.	A

21.	D
22.	A
23.	C
24.	B
25.	B

———

TEST 2

DIRECTIONS: Each question or incomplete statement is followed by several suggested answers or completions. Select the one that BEST answers the question or completes the statement. *PRINT THE LETTER OF THE CORRECT ANSWER IN THE SPACE AT THE RIGHT.*

1. Of the following, the MOST appropriate manner for an interviewer to assume during an interview with a client is   1.____

   A. authoritarian   B. paternal   C. casual   D. businesslike

2. The systematic study of interviewing theory, principles and techniques by an interviewer will, *usually*   2.____

   A. aid him to act in a depersonalized manner
   B. turn his interviewes into stereotyped affairs
   C. make the people he interviews feel manipulated
   D. give him a basis for critically examining his own practice

3. Compiling in advance a list of general questions to ask a client during an interview is a technique *usually* considered   3.____

   A. *desirable,* chiefly because reference to the list will help keep the interview focused on the important issues
   B. *undesirable,* chiefly because use of such a list will discourage the client from speaking freely
   C. *desirable,* chiefly because the list will serve as a record of what questions were asked
   D. *undesirable,* chiefly because use of such a list will make the interview too mechanical and impersonal

4. The one of the following which is usually of GREATEST importance in winning the cooperation of a person being interviewed while achieving the purpose of the interview is the interviewer's ability to   4.____

   A. gain the confidence of the person being interviewed
   B. stick to the subject of the interview
   C. handle a person who is obviously lying
   D. prevent the person being interviewed from withholding information

5. While interviewing clients, an interviewer should use the technique of interruption, beginning to speak when a client has temporarily paused at the end of a phrase or sentence, in order to   5.____

   A. limit the client's ability to voice his objections or complaints
   B. shorten, terminate or redirect a client's response
   C. assert authority when he feels that the client is too conceited
   D. demonstrate to the client that pauses in speech should be avoided

6. An interviewer might gain background information about a client by being aware of the person's speech during an interview.
   Which one of the following patterns of speech would offer the LEAST accurate information about a client? The   6.____

A. number of slang expressions and the level of vocabulary
B. presence and degree of an accent
C. rate of speech and the audibility level
D. presence of a physical speech defect

7. Suppose that you are interviewing a distressed client who claims that he was just laid off from his job and has no money to pay his rent.
Your FIRST action should be to

   7.____

A. ask if he has sought other employment or has other sources of income
B. express your sympathy but explain that he must pay the rent on time
C. inquire about the reasons he was laid off from work
D. try to transfer him to a smaller apartment which he can afford

8. Suppose you have some background information on an applicant whom you are interviewing. During the interview it appears that the applicant is giving you *false* information. The BEST thing for you to do at that point is to

   8.____

A. pretend that you are not aware of the written facts and let him continue
B. tell him what you already know and discuss the discrepancies with him
C. terminate the interview and make a note that the applicant is untrustworthy
D. tell him that, because he is making false statements, he will not be eligible for an apartment

9. A Spanish-speaking applicant may want to bring his bilingual child with him to an interview to act as an interpreter. Which of the following would be LEAST likely to affect the value of an interview in which an applicant 's child has acted as interpreter?

   9.____

A. It may make it undesirable to ask certain questions.
B. A child may do an inadequate job of interpretation.
C. A child 's answers may indicate his feelings toward his parents.
D. The applicant may not want to reveal all information in front of his child.

10. Assume you are assigned to interview applicants.
Of the following, which is the BEST attitude for you to take in dealing with applicants?

   10.____

A. Assume they will enjoy being interviewed because they believe that you have the power of decision
B. Expect that they have a history of anti-social behavior in the family, and probe deeply into the social development of family members
C. Expect that they will try to control the interview, thus you should keep them on the defensive
D. Assume that they will be polite and cooperative and attempt to secure the information you need in a business-like manner

11. If you are interviewing an applicant who is a minority group member in reference to his eligibility, it would be BEST for you to use language that is

   11.____

A. *informal,* using ethnic expressions known to the applicant
B. *technical,* using the expressions commonly used in the agency
C. *simple,* using words and phrases which laymen understand
D. *formal,* to remind the applicant that he is dealing with a government agency

12. When interviewing an applicant to determine his eligibility, it is MOST important to   12._____

    A. have a prior mental picture of the typical eligible applicant
    B. conduct the interview strictly according to a previously prepared script
    C. keep in mind the goal of the interview, which is to determine eligibility
    D. get an accurate and detailed account of the applicant's life history

13. The practice of trying to imagine yourself in the applicant's place during an interview is   13._____

    A. *good;* mainly because you will be able to evaluate his responses better
    B. *good;* mainly because it will enable you to treat him as a friend rather than as an applicant
    C. *poor;* mainly because it is important for the applicant to see you as an impartial person
    D. *poor;* mainly because it is too time-consuming to do this with each applicant

14. When dealing with clients from different ethnic backgrounds, you should be aware of cer-   14._____
tain tendencies toward prejudice.
Which of the following statements is LEAST likely to be valid?

    A. Whites prejudiced against blacks are more likely to be prejudiced against Hispanics than whites not prejudiced against blacks.
    B. The less a white is in competition with blacks, the less likely he is to be prejudiced against them.
    C. Persons who have moved from one social group to another are likely to retain the attitudes and prejudices of their original social group.
    D. When there are few blacks or Hispanics in a project, whites are less likely to be prejudiced against them than when there are many.

15. Of the following, the one who is MOST likely to be a good interviewer of people seeking   15._____
assistance, is one who

    A. tries to get applicants to apply to another agency instead
    B. believes that it is necessary to get as much pertinent information as possible in order to determine the applicant's real needs
    C. believes that people who seek assistance are likely to have persons with a history of irresponsible behavior in their households
    D. is convinced that there is no need for a request for assistance

---

KEYS (CORRECT ANSWERS)

1. D
2. D
3. A
4. A
5. B

6. C
7. A
8. B
9. C
10. D

11. C
12. C
13. A
14. C
15. B

Evaluating Conclusions in Light of Known Facts

EXAMINATION SECTION
TEST 1

DIRECTIONS: Each question or incomplete statement is followed by several suggested answers or completions. Select the one that BEST answers the question or completes the statement. *PRINT THE LETTER OF THE CORRECT ANSWER IN THE SPACE AT THE RIGHT.*

Questions 1-9.

DIRECTIONS: In questions 1-9, you will read a set of facts and a conclusion drawn from them. The conclusion may be valid or invalid, based on the facts—it's your task to determine the validity of the conclusion.

For each question, select the letter before the statement that BEST expresses the relationship between the given facts and the conclusion that has been drawn from them. Your choices are:
A. The facts prove the conclusion
B. The facts disprove the conclusion; or
C. The facts neither prove nor disprove the conclusion.

1. FACTS: If the supervisor retires, James, the assistant supervisor, will not be transferred to another department. James will be promoted to supervisor if he is not transferred. The supervisor retired.

   CONCLUSION: James will be promoted to supervisor.

   A. The facts prove the conclusion.
   B. The facts disprove the conclusion.
   C. The facts neither prove nor disprove the conclusion.

1.____

2. FACTS: In the town of Luray, every player on the softball team works at Luray National Bank. In addition, every player on the Luray softball team wears glasses.

   CONCLUSION: At least some of the people who work at Luray National Bank wear glasses.

   A. The facts prove the conclusion.
   B. The facts disprove the conclusion.
   C. The facts neither prove nor disprove the conclusion.

2.____

3. FACTS: The only time Henry and June go out to dinner is on an evening when they have childbirth classes. Their childbirth classes meet on Tuesdays and Thursdays.

   CONCLUSION: Henry and June never go out to dinner on Friday or Saturday.

   A. The facts prove the conclusion.
   B. The facts disprove the conclusion.
   C. The facts neither prove nor disprove the conclusion.

3.____

73

4. FACTS: Every player on the field hockey team has at least one bruise. Everyone on the field hockey team also has scarred knees.

   CONCLUSION: Most people with both bruises and scarred knees are field hockey players.

   A. The facts prove the conclusion.
   B. The facts disprove the conclusion.
   C. The facts neither prove nor disprove the conclusion.

   4.____

5. FACTS: In the chess tournament, Lance will win his match against Jane if Jane wins her match against Mathias. If Lance wins his match against Jane, Christine will not win her match against Jane.

   CONCLUSION: Christine will not win her match against Jane if Jane wins her match against Mathias.

   A. The facts prove the conclusion.
   B. The facts disprove the conclusion.
   C. The facts neither prove nor disprove the conclusion.

   5.____

6. FACTS: No green lights on the machine are indicators for the belt drive status. Not all of the lights on the machine's upper panel are green. Some lights on the machine's lower panel are green.

   CONCLUSION: The green lights on the machine's lower panel may be indicators for the belt drive status.

   A. The facts prove the conclusion.
   B. The facts disprove the conclusion.
   C. The facts neither prove nor disprove the conclusion.

   6.____

7. FACTS: At a small, one-room country school, there are eight students: Amy, Ben, Carla, Dan, Elliot, Francine, Greg, and Hannah. Each student is in either the 6th, 7th, or 8th grade. Either two or three students are in each grade. Amy, Dan, and Francine are all in different grades. Ben and Elliot are both in the 7th grade. Hannah and Carl are in the same grade.

   CONCLUSION: Exactly three students are in the 7th grade.

   A. The facts prove the conclusion.
   B. The facts disprove the conclusion.
   C. The facts neither prove nor disprove the conclusion.

   7.____

8. FACTS: Two married couples are having lunch together. Two of the four people are German and two are Russian, but in each couple the nationality of a spouse is not necessarily the same as the other's. One person in the group is a teacher, the other a lawyer, one an engineer, and the other a writer. The teacher is a Russian man. The writer is Russian, and her husband is an engineer. One of the people, Mr. Stern, is German.

   CONCLUSION: Mr. Stern's wife is a writer.

   8.____

A. The facts prove the conclusion.
B. The facts disprove the conclusion.
C. The facts neither prove nor disprove the conclusion.

9. FACTS: The flume ride at the county fair is open only to children who are at least 36 inches tall. Lisa is 30 inches tall. John is shorter than Henry, but more than 10 inches taller than Lisa.

9.____

CONCLUSION: Lisa is the only one who can't ride the flume ride.

A. The facts prove the conclusion.
B. The facts disprove the conclusion.
C. The facts neither prove nor disprove the conclusion.

Questions 10-17.

DIRECTIONS: Questions 10-17 are based on the following reading passage. It is not your knowledge of the particular topic that is being tested, but your ability to reason based on what you have read. The passage is likely to detail several proposed courses of action and factors affecting these proposals. The reading passage is followed by a conclusion or outcome based on the facts in the passage, or a description of a decision taken regarding the situation. The conclusion is followed by a number of statements that have a possible connection to the conclusion. For each statement, you are to determine whether:

A. The statement proves the conclusion.
B. The statement supports the conclusion but does not prove it.
C. The statement disproves the conclusion.
D. The statement weakens the conclusion but does not disprove it.
E. The statement has no relevance to the conclusion.

Remember that the conclusion after the passage is to be accepted as the outcome of what actually happened, and that you are being asked to evaluate the impact each statement would have had on the conclusion.

PASSAGE:

The Grand Army of Foreign Wars, a national veteran's organization, is struggling to maintain its National Home, where the widowed spouses and orphans of deceased members are housed together in a small village-like community. The Home is open to spouses and children who are bereaved for any reason, regardless of whether the member's death was related to military service, but a new global conflict has led to a dramatic surge in the number of members' deaths: many veterans who re-enlisted for the conflict have been killed in action.

The Grand Army of Foreign Wars is considering several options for handling the increased number of applications for housing at the National Home, which has been traditionally supported by membership dues. At its national convention, it will choose only one of the following:

The first idea is a one-time $50 tax on all members, above and beyond the dues they pay already. Since the organization has more than a million members, this tax should be sufficient for the construction and maintenance of new housing for applicants on the existing grounds of the National Home. The idea is opposed, however, by some older members who live on fixed incomes. These members object in principle to the taxation of Grand Army members. The Grand Army has never imposed a tax on its members.

The second idea is to launch a national fund-raising drive and public relations campaign that will attract donations for the National Home. Several national celebrities are members of the organization, and other celebrities could be attracted to the cause. Many Grand Army members are wary of this approach, however: in the past, the net receipts of some fund-raising efforts have been relatively insignificant, given the costs of staging them.

A third approach, suggested by many of the younger members, is to have new applicants share some of the costs of construction and maintenance. The spouses and children would pay an up-front "enrollment" fee, based on a sliding scale proportionate to their income and assets, and then a monthly fee adjusted similarly to contribute to maintenance costs. Many older members are strongly opposed to this idea, as it is in direct contradiction to the principles on which the organization was founded more than a century ago.

The fourth option is simply to maintain the status quo, focus the organization's efforts on supporting the families who already live at the National Home, and wait to accept new applicants based on attrition.

CONCLUSION: At its annual national convention, the Grand Army of Foreign Wars votes to impose a one-time tax of $10 on each member for the purpose of expanding and supporting the National Home to welcome a larger number of applicants. The tax is considered to be the solution most likely to produce the funds needed to accommodate the growing number of applicants.

10. Actuarial studies have shown that because the Grand Army's membership consists mostly of older veterans from earlier wars, the organization's membership will suffer a precipitous decline in numbers in about five years.

    10.____

    A.
    B.
    C.
    D.
    E.

11. After passage of the funding measure, a splinter group of older members appeals for the "sliding scale" provision to be applied to the tax, so that some members may be allowed to contribute less based on their income.

    11.____

    A.
    B.
    C.
    D.
    E.

12. The original charter of the Grand Army of Foreign Wars specifically states that the orga-   12._____
    nization will not levy any taxes or duties on its members beyond its modest annual dues.
    It takes a super-majority of attending delegates at the national convention to make alter-
    ations to the charter.

    A.
    B.
    C.
    D.
    E.

13. Six months before Grand Army of Foreign Wars'national convention, the Internal Reve-   13._____
    nue Service rules that because it is an organization that engages in political lobbying, the
    Grand Army must no longer enjoy its own federal tax-exempt status.

    A.
    B.
    C.
    D.
    E.

14. Two months before the national convention, Dirk Rockwell, arguably the country's most   14._____
    famous film actor, announces in a nationally televised interview that he has been sad-
    dened to learn of the plight of the National Home, and that he is going to make it his own
    personal crusade to see that it is able to house and support a greater number of wid-
    owed spouses and orphans in the future.

    A.
    B.
    C.
    D.
    E.

15. The Grand Army's final estimate is that the cost of expanding the National Home to   15._____
    accommodate the increased number of applicants will be about $61 million.

    A.
    B.
    C.
    D.
    E.

16. Just before the national convention, the federal Department of Veterans Affairs   16._____
    announces steep cuts in the benefits package that is currently offered to the widowed
    spouses and orphans of veterans.

    A.
    B.
    C.
    D.

17. After the national convention, the Grand Army of Foreign Wars begins charging a modest   17.____
    "start-up" fee to all families who apply for residence at the national home.

    A.
    B.
    C.
    D.
    E.

Questions 18-25.

DIRECTIONS: Questions 18-25 each provide four factual statements and a conclusion based
on these statements. After reading the entire question, you will decide
whether:
    A. The conclusion is proved by statements 1-4;
    B. The conclusion is disproved by statements 1-4; or
    C. The facts are not sufficient to prove or disprove the conclusion.

18. FACTUAL STATEMENTS: 18.____

1. In the Field Day high jump competition, Martha jumped higher than Frank.
2. Carl jumped higher than Ignacio.
3. Ignacio jumped higher than Frank.
4. Dan jumped higher than Carl.

CONCLUSION: Frank finished last in the high jump competition.

    A. The conclusion is proved by statements 1-4.
    B. The conclusion is disproved by statements 1-4.
    C. The facts are not sufficient to prove or disprove the conclusion.

19. FACTUAL STATEMENTS: 19.____

1. The door to the hammer mill chamber is locked if light 6 is red.
2. The door to the hammer mill chamber is locked only when the mill is operating.
3. If the mill is not operating, light 6 is blue.
4. Light 6 is blue.

CONCLUSION: The door to the hammer mill chamber is locked.

    A. The conclusion is proved by statements 1-4.
    B. The conclusion is disproved by statements 1-4.
    C. The facts are not sufficient to prove or disprove the conclusion.

20. **FACTUAL STATEMENTS:**   20._____

   1. Ziegfried, the lion tamer at the circus, has demanded ten additional minutes of performance time during each show.
   2. If Ziegfried is allowed his ten additional minutes per show, he will attempt to teach Kimba the tiger to shoot a basketball.
   3. If Kimba learns how to shoot a basketball, then Ziegfried was not given his ten additional minutes.
   4. Ziegfried was given his ten additional minutes.

   CONCLUSION: Despite Ziegfried's efforts, Kimba did not learn how to shoot a basketball.

   A. The conclusion is proved by statements 1-4.
   B. The conclusion is disproved by statements 1-4.
   C. The facts are not sufficient to prove or disprove the conclusion.

21. **FACTUAL STATEMENTS:**   21._____

   1. If Stan goes to counseling, Sara won't divorce him.
   2. If Sara divorces Stan, she'll move back to Texas.
   3. If Sara doesn't divorce Stan, Irene will be disappointed.
   4. Stan goes to counseling.

   CONCLUSION: Irene will be disappointed.

   A. The conclusion is proved by statements 1-4.
   B. The conclusion is disproved by statements 1-4.
   C. The facts are not sufficient to prove or disprove the conclusion.

22. **FACTUAL STATEMENTS:**   22._____

   1. If Delia is promoted to district manager, Claudia will have to be promoted to team leader.
   2. Delia will be promoted to district manager unless she misses her fourth-quarter sales quota.
   3. If Claudia is promoted to team leader, Thomas will be promoted to assistant team leader.
   4. Delia meets her fourth-quarter sales quota.

   CONCLUSION: Thomas is promoted to assistant team leader.

   A. The conclusion is proved by statements 1-4.
   B. The conclusion is disproved by statements 1-4.
   C. The facts are not sufficient to prove or disprove the conclusion.

23. **FACTUAL STATEMENTS:**   23.____

    1. Clone D is identical to Clone B.
    2. Clone B is not identical to Clone A.
    3. Clone D is not identical to Clone C.
    4. Clone E is not identical to the clones that are identical to Clone B.

    CONCLUSION: Clone E is identical to Clone D.

    A. The conclusion is proved by statements 1-4.
    B. The conclusion is disproved by statements 1-4.
    C. The facts are not sufficient to prove or disprove the conclusion.

24. **FACTUAL STATEMENTS:**   24.____

    1. In the Stafford Tower, each floor is occupied by a single business.
    2. Big G Staffing is on a floor between CyberGraphics and MainEvent.
    3. Gasco is on the floor directly below CyberGraphics and three floors above Treehorn Audio.
    4. MainEvent is five floors below EZ Tax and four floors below Treehorn Audio.

    CONCLUSION: EZ Tax is on a floor between Gasco and MainEvent.

    A. The conclusion is proved by statements 1-4.
    B. The conclusion is disproved by statements 1-4.
    C. The facts are not sufficient to prove or disprove the conclusion.

25. **FACTUAL STATEMENTS:**   25.____

    1. Only county roads lead to Nicodemus.
    2. All the roads from Hill City to Graham County are federal highways.
    3. Some of the roads from Plainville lead to Nicodemus.
    4. Some of the roads running from Hill City lead to Strong City.

    CONCLUSION: Some of the roads from Plainville are county roads.

    A. The conclusion is proved by statements 1-4.
    B. The conclusion is disproved by statements 1-4.
    C. The facts are not sufficient to prove or disprove the conclusion.

KEY (CORRECT ANSWERS)

1.	A		11.	A
2.	A		12.	D
3.	A		13.	E
4.	C		14.	D
5.	A		15.	B
6.	B		16.	B
7.	A		17.	C
8.	A		18.	A
9.	A		19.	B
10.	E		20.	A

21.	A
22.	A
23.	B
24.	A
25.	A

SOLUTIONS TO PROBLEMS

1) (A) Given statement 3, we deduce that James will not be transferred to another department. By statement 2, we can conclude that James will be promoted.

2) (A) Since every player on the softball team wears glasses, these individuals compose some of the people who work at the bank. Although not every person who works at the bank plays softball, those bank employees who do play softball wear glasses.

3) (A) If Henry and June go out to dinner, we conclude that it must be on Tuesday or Thursday, which are the only two days when they have childbirth classes. This implies that if it is not Tuesday or Thursday, then this couple does not go out to dinner.

4) (C) We can only conclude that if a person plays on the field hockey team, then he or she has both bruises and scarred knees. But there are probably a great number of people who have both bruises and scarred knees but do not play on the field hockey team. The given conclusion can neither be proven or disproven.

5) (A) From statement 1, if Jane beats Mathias, then Lance will beat Jane. Using statement 2, we can then conclude that Christine will not win her match against Jane.

6) (B) Statement 1 tells us that no green light can be an indicator of the belt drive status. Thus, the given conclusion must be false.

7) (A) We already know that Ben and Elliot are in the 7th grade. Even though Hannah and Carl are in the same grade, it cannot be the 7th grade because we would then have at least four students in this 7th grade. This would contradict the third statement, which states that either two or three students are in each grade. Since Amy, Dan, and Francine are in different grades, exactly one of them must be in the 7th grade. Thus, Ben, Elliot and exactly one of Amy, Dan, and Francine are the three students in the 7th grade.

8) (A) One man is a teacher, who is Russian. We know that the writer is female and is Russian. Since her husband is an engineer, he cannot be the Russian teacher. Thus, her husband is of German descent, namely Mr. Stern. This means that Mr. Stern's wife is the writer. Note that one couple consists of a male Russian teacher and a female German lawyer. The other couple consists of a male German engineer and a female Russian writer.

9) (A) Since John is more than 10 inches taller than Lisa, his height is at least 46 inches. Also, John is shorter than Henry, so Henry's height must be greater than 46 inches. Thus, Lisa is the only one whose height is less than 36 inches. Therefore, she is the only one who is not allowed on the flume ride.

18) (A) Dan jumped higher than Carl, who jumped higher than Ignacio, who jumped higher than Frank. Since Martha jumped higher than Frank, every person jumped higher than Frank. Thus, Frank finished last.

19) (B) If the light is red, then the door is locked. If the door is locked, then the mill is operating. Reversing the logical sequence of these statements, if the mill is not operating, then the door is not locked, which means that the light is blue. Thus, the given conclusion is disproved.

20) (A) Using the contrapositive of statement 3, if Ziegfried was given his ten additional minutes, then Kimba did not learn how to shoot a basketball. Since statement 4 is factual, the conclusion is proved.

21) (A) From statements 4 and 1, we conclude that Sara doesn't divorce Stan. Then statement 3 reveals that Irene will be disappointed. Thus the conclusion is proved.

22) (A) Statement 2 can be rewritten as "Delia is promoted to district manager or she misses her sales quota." Furthermore, this statement is equivalent to "If Delia makes her sales quota, then she is promoted to district manager." From statement 1, we conclude that Claudia is promoted to team leader. Finally, by statement 3, Thomas is promoted to assistant team leader. The conclusion is proved.

23) (B) By statement 4, Clone E is not identical to any clones identical to clone B. Statement 1 tells us that clones B and D are identical. Therefore, clone E cannot be identical to clone D. The conclusion is disproved.

24) (A) Based on all four statements, CyberGraphics is somewhere below Main Event. Gasco is one floor below CyberGraphics. EZ Tax is two floors below Gasco. Treehorn Audio is one floor below EZ Tax. Main Event is four floors below Treehorn Audio. Thus, EZ Tax is two floors below Gasco and five floors above Main Event. The conclusion is proved.

25) (A) From statement 3, we know that some of the roads from Plainville lead to Nicodemus. But statement 1 tells us that only county roads lead to Nicodemus. Therefore, some of the roads from Plainville must be county roads. The conclusion is proved.

TEST 2

DIRECTIONS: Each question or incomplete statement is followed by several suggested answers or completions. Select the one that BEST answers the question or completes the statement. *PRINT THE LETTER OF THE CORRECT ANSWER IN THE SPACE AT THE RIGHT.*

Questions 1-9.

DIRECTIONS: In questions 1-9, you will read a set of facts and a conclusion drawn from them. The conclusion may be valid or invalid, based on the facts-it's your task to determine the validity of the conclusion.

For each question, select the letter before the statement that BEST expresses the relationship between the given facts and the conclusion that has been drawn from them. Your choices are:
A.   The facts prove the conclusion
B.   The facts disprove the conclusion; or
C.   The facts neither prove nor disprove the conclusion.

1.   FACTS: Some employees in the testing department are statisticians. Most of the statisticians who work in the testing department are projection specialists. Tom Wilks works in the testing department.

    CONCLUSION: Tom Wilks is a statistician.

    A.   The facts prove the conclusion.
    B.   The facts disprove the conclusion.
    C.   The facts neither prove nor disprove the conclusion.

    1.____

2.   FACTS: Ten coins are split among Hank, Lawrence, and Gail. If Lawrence gives his coins to Hank, then Hank will have more coins than Gail. If Gail gives her coins to Lawrence, then Lawrence will have more coins than Hank.

    CONCLUSION: Hank has six coins.

    A.   The facts prove the conclusion.
    B.   The facts disprove the conclusion.
    C.   The facts neither prove nor disprove the conclusion.

    2.____

3.   FACTS: Nobody loves everybody. Janet loves Ken. Ken loves everybody who loves Janet.

    CONCLUSION: Everybody loves Janet.

    A.   The facts prove the conclusion.
    B.   The facts disprove the conclusion.
    C.   The facts neither prove nor disprove the conclusion.

    3.____

4. FACTS: Most of the Torres family lives in East Los Angeles. Many people in East Los Angeles celebrate Cinco de Mayo. Joe is a member of the Torres family.

4.____

CONCLUSION: Joe lives in East Los Angeles.

   A. The facts prove the conclusion.
   B. The facts disprove the conclusion.
   C. The facts neither prove nor disprove the conclusion.

5. FACTS: Five professionals each occupy one story of a five-story office building. Dr. Kane's office is above Dr. Assad's. Dr. Johnson's office is between Dr. Kane's and Dr. Conlon's. Dr. Steen's office is between Dr. Conlon's and Dr. Assad's. Dr. Johnson is on the fourth story.

5.____

CONCLUSION: Dr. Kane occupies the top story.

   A. The facts prove the conclusion.
   B. The facts disprove the conclusion.
   C. The facts neither prove nor disprove the conclusion.

6. FACTS: To be eligible for membership in the Yukon Society, a person must be able to either tunnel through a snowbank while wearing only a T-shirt and shorts, or hold his breath for two minutes under water that is 50° F. Ray can only hold his breath for a minute and a half.

6.____

CONCLUSION: Ray can still become a member of the Yukon Society by tunneling through a snowbank while wearing a T-shirt and shorts.

   A. The facts prove the conclusion.
   B. The facts disprove the conclusion.
   C. The facts neither prove nor disprove the conclusion.

7. FACTS: A mark is worth five plunks. You can exchange four sharps for a tinplot. It takes eight marks to buy a sharp.

7.____

CONCLUSION: A sharp is the most valuable.

   A. The facts prove the conclusion.
   B. The facts disprove the conclusion.
   C. The facts neither prove nor disprove the conclusion.

8. FACTS: There are gibbons, as well as lemurs, who like to play in the trees at the monkey house. All those who like to play in the trees at the monkey house are fed lettuce and bananas.

8.____

CONCLUSION: Lemurs and gibbons are types of monkeys.

   A. The facts prove the conclusion.
   B. The facts disprove the conclusion.
   C. The facts neither prove nor disprove the conclusion.

9. FACTS: None of the Blackfoot tribes is a Salishan Indian tribe. Sal-ishan Indians came   9.____
from the northern Pacific Coast. All Salishan Indians live east of the Continental Divide.

CONCLUSION: No Blackfoot tribes live east of the Continental Divide.

   A.   The facts prove the conclusion.
   B.   The facts disprove the conclusion.
   C.   The facts neither prove nor disprove the conclusion.

Questions 10-17.

DIRECTIONS: Questions 10-17 are based on the following reading passage. It is not your knowledge of the particular topic that is being tested, but your ability to reason based on what you have read. The passage is likely to detail several proposed courses of action and factors affecting these proposals. The reading passage is followed by a conclusion or outcome based on the facts in the passage, or a description of a decision taken regarding the situation. The conclusion is fol-lowed by a number of statements that have a possible connection to the con-clusion. For each statement, you are to determine whether:

   A.   The statement proves the conclusion.
   B.   The statement supports the conclusion but does not prove it.
   C.   The statement disproves the conclusion.
   D.   The statement weakens the conclusion but does not disprove it.
   E.   The statement has no relevance to the conclusion.

Remember that the conclusion after the passage is to be accepted as the outcome of what actually happened, and that you are being asked to evaluate the impact each state-ment would have had on the conclusion.

PASSAGE:

On August 12, Beverly Willey reported that she was in the elevator late on the previous evening after leaving her office on the 16th floor of a large office building. In her report, she states that a man got on the elevator at the 11th floor, pulled her off the elevator, assaulted her, and stole her purse. Ms. Willey reported that she had seen the man in the elevators and hallways of the building before. She believes that the man works in the building. Her description of him is as follows: he is tall, unshaven, with wavy brown hair and a scar on his left cheek. He walks with a pronounced limp, often dragging his left foot behind his right.

CONCLUSION: After Beverly Willey makes her report, the police arrest a 43-year-man, Barton Black, and charge him with her assault.

10. Barton Black is a former Marine who served in Vietnam, where he sustained shrapnel   10.____
wounds to the left side of his face and suffered nerve damage in his left leg.

   A.
   B.
   C.
   D.
   E.

11. When they arrived at his residence to question him, detectives were greeted at the door by Barton Black, who was tall and clean-shaven.   11.____

    A.
    B.
    C.
    D.
    E.

12. Barton Black was booked into the county jail several days after Beverly Willey's assault.   12.____

    A.
    B.
    C.
    D.
    E.

13. Upon further investigation, detectives discover that Beverly Willey does not work at the office building.   13.____

    A.
    B.
    C.
    D.
    E.

14. Upon further investigation, detectives discover that Barton Black does not work at the office building.   14.____

    A.
    B.
    C.
    D.
    E.

15. In the spring of the following year, Barton Black is convicted of assaulting Beverly Willey on August 11.   15.____

    A.
    B.
    C.
    D.
    E.

16. During their investigation of the assault, detectives determine that Beverly Willey was assaulted on the 12th floor of the office building.   16.____

    A.
    B.
    C.
    D.
    E.

17. The day after Beverly Willey's assault, Barton Black fled the area and was never seen   17._____
    again.

    A.
    B.
    C.
    D.
    E.

Questions 18-25.

DIRECTIONS: Questions 18-25 each provide four factual statements and a conclusion based
              on these statements. After reading the entire question, you will decide
              whether:

              A.   The conclusion is proved by statements 1-4;
              B.   The conclusion is disproved by statements 1-4; or
              C.   The facts are not sufficient to prove or disprove the conclusion.

18. FACTUAL STATEMENTS: 18._____

     1. Among five spice jars on the shelf, the sage is to the right of the parsley.
     2. The pepper is to the left of the basil.
     3. The nutmeg is between the sage and the pepper.
     4. The pepper is the second spice from the left.

     CONCLUSION: The sage is the farthest to the right.

     A.   The conclusion is proved by statements 1-4.
     B.   The conclusion is disproved by statements 1-4.
     C.   The facts are not sufficient to prove or disprove the conclusion.

19. FACTUAL STATEMENTS: 19._____

     1. Gear X rotates in a clockwise direction if Switch C is in the OFF position
     2. Gear X will rotate in a counter-clockwise direction if Switch C is ON.
     3. If Gear X is rotating in a clockwise direction, then Gear Y will not be rotating at all.
     4. Switch C is ON.

     CONCLUSION: Gear X is rotating in a counter-clockwise direction.

     A.   The conclusion is proved by statements 1-4.
     B.   The conclusion is disproved by statements 1-4.
     C.   The facts are not sufficient to prove or disprove the conclusion.

20. **FACTUAL STATEMENTS:**
    1. Lane will leave for the Toronto meeting today only if Terence, Rourke, and Jackson all file their marketing reports by the end of the work day.
    2. Rourke will file her report on time only if Ganz submits last quarter's data.
    3. If Terence attends the security meeting, he will attend it with Jackson, and they will not file their marketing reports by the end of the work day.
    4. Ganz submits last quarter's data to Rourke.

    CONCLUSION: Lane will leave for the Toronto meeting today.

    A. The conclusion is proved by statements 1-4.
    B. The conclusion is disproved by statements 1-4.
    C. The facts are not sufficient to prove or disprove the conclusion.

21. **FACTUAL STATEMENTS:**

    1. Bob is in second place in the Boston Marathon.
    2. Gregory is winning the Boston Marathon.
    3. There are four miles to go in the race, and Bob is gaining on Gregory at the rate of 100 yards every minute.
    4. There are 1760 yards in a mile, and Gregory's usual pace during the Boston Marathon is one mile every six minutes.

    CONCLUSION: Bob wins the Boston Marathon.

    A. The conclusion is proved by statements 1-4.
    B. The conclusion is disproved by statements 1-4.
    C. The facts are not sufficient to prove or disprove the conclusion.

22. **FACTUAL STATEMENTS:**

    1. Four brothers are named Earl, John, Gary, and Pete.
    2. Earl and Pete are unmarried.
    3. John is shorter than the youngest of the four.
    4. The oldest brother is married, and is also the tallest.

    CONCLUSION: Gary is the oldest brother.

    A. The conclusion is proved by statements 1-4.
    B. The conclusion is disproved by statements 1-4.
    C. The facts are not sufficient to prove or disprove the conclusion.

23. **FACTUAL STATEMENTS:**

    1. Brigade X is ten miles from the demilitarized zone.
    2. If General Woundwort gives the order, Brigade X will advance to the demilitarized zone, but not quickly enough to reach the zone before the conflict begins.
    3. Brigade Y, five miles behind Brigade X, will not advance unless General Woundwort gives the order.
    4. Brigade Y advances.

    CONCLUSION: Brigade X reaches the demilitarized zone before the conflict begins.

A. The conclusion is proved by statements 1-4.
B. The conclusion is disproved by statements 1-4.
C. The facts are not sufficient to prove or disprove the conclusion.

24. FACTUAL STATEMENTS:

24.____

1. Jerry has decided to take a cab from Fullerton to Elverton.
2. Chubby Cab charges $5 plus $3 a mile.
3. Orange Cab charges $7.50 but gives free mileage for the first 5 miles.
4. After the first 5 miles, Orange Cab charges $2.50 a mile.

CONCLUSION: Orange Cab is the cheaper fare from Fullerton to Elverton.

A. The conclusion is proved by statements 1-4.
B. The conclusion is disproved by statements 1-4.
C. The facts are not sufficient to prove or disprove the conclusion.

25. FACTUAL STATEMENTS:

25.____

1. Dan is never in class when his friend Lucy is absent.
2. Lucy is never absent unless her mother is sick.
3. If Lucy is in class, Sergio is in class also
4. Sergio is never in class when Dalton is absent.

CONCLUSION: If Lucy is absent, Dalton may be in class.

A. The conclusion is proved by statements 1-4.
B. The conclusion is disproved by statements 1-4.
C. The facts are not sufficient to prove or disprove the conclusion.

KEY (CORRECT ANSWERS)

1.	C		11.	E
2.	B		12.	B
3.	B		13.	D
4.	C		14.	E
5.	A		15.	A
6.	A		16.	E
7.	B		17.	C
8.	C		18.	B
9.	C		19.	A
10.	B		20.	C

21.	C
22.	A
23.	B
24.	A
25.	B

SOLUTIONS TO PROBLEMS

1) (C) Statement 1 only tells us that some employees who work in the Testing Department are statisticians. This means that we need to allow the possibility that at least one person in this department is not a statistician. Thus, if a person works in the Testing Department, we cannot conclude whether or not this individual is a statistician.

2) (B) If Hank had six coins, then the total of Gails collection and Lawrence's collection would be four. Thus, if Gail gave all her coins to Lawrence, Lawrence would only have four coins. Thus, it would be impossible for Lawrence to have more coins than Hank.

3) (B) Statement 1 tells us that nobody loves everybody. If everybody loved Janet, then Statement 3 would imply that Ken loves everybody. This would contradict statement 1. The conclusion is disproved.

4) (C) Although most of the Torres family lives in East Los Angeles, we can assume that some members of this family do not live in East Los Angeles. Thus, we cannot prove or disprove that Joe, who is a member of the Torres family, lives in East Los Angeles.

5) (A) Since Dr. Johnson is on the 4th floor, either (a) Dr. Kane is on the 5th floor and Dr. Conlon is on the 3rd floor, or (b) Dr. Kane is on the 3rd floor and Dr. Conlon is on the 5th floor. If option (b) were correct, then since Dr. Assad would be on the 1st floor, it would be impossible for Dr. Steen's office to be between Dr. Conlon and Dr. Assad's office. Therefore, Dr. Kane's office must be on the 5th floor. The order of the doctors' offices, from 5th floor down to the 1st floor is: Dr. Kane, Dr. Johnson, Dr. Conlon, Dr. Steen, Dr. Assad.

6) (A) Ray does not satisfy the requirement of holding his breath for two minutes under water, since he can only hold his breath for one minute in that setting. But if he tunnels through a snowbank with just a T-shirt and shorts, he will satisfy the eligibility requirement. Note that the eligibility requirement contains the key word "or." So only one of the two clauses separated by "or" need to be fulfilled.

7) (B) Statement 2 says that four sharps is equivalent to one tinplot. This means that a tinplot is worth more than a sharp. The conclusion is disproved. We note that the order of these items, from most valuable to least valuable are: tinplot, sharp, mark, plunk.

8) (C) We can only conclude that gibbons and lemurs are fed lettuce and bananas. We can neither prove or disprove that these animals are types of monkeys.

9) (C) We know that all Salishan Indians live east of the Continental Divide. But some nonmembers of this tribe of Indians may also live east of the Continental Divide. Since none of the members of the Blackfoot tribe belong to the Salishan Indian tribe, we cannot draw any conclusion about the location of the Blackfoot tribe with respect to the Continental Divide.

18) (B) Since the pepper is second from the left and the nutmeg is between the sage and the pepper, the positions 2, 3, and 4 (from the left) are pepper, nutmeg, sage. By statement 2, the basil must be in position 5, which implies that the parsley is in position 1. Therefore, the basil, not the sage is farthest to the right. The conclusion disproved.

19) (A) Statement 2 assures us that if switch C is ON, then Gear X is rotating in a counterclockwise direction. The conclusion is proved.

20) (C) Based on Statement 4, followed by Statement 2, we conclude that Ganz and Rourke will file their reports on time. Statement 3 reveals that if Terence and Jackson attend the security meeting, they will fail to file their reports on time. We have no further information if Terence and Jackson attended the security meeting, so we are not able to either confirm or deny that their reports were filed on time. This implies that we cannot know for certain that Lane will leave for his meeting in Toronto.

21) (C) Although Bob is in second place behind Gregory, we cannot deduce how far behind Gregory he is running. At Gregory's current pace, he will cover four miles in 24 minutes. If Bob were only 100 yards behind Gregory, he would catch up to Gregory in one minute. But if Bob were very far behind Gregory, for example 5 miles, this is the equivalent of (5)(1760) = 8800 yards. Then Bob would need 8800/100 = 88 minutes to catch up to Gregory. Thus, the given facts are not sufficient to draw a conclusion.

22) (A) Statement 2 tells us that neither Earl nor Pete could be the oldest; also, either John or Gary is married. Statement 4 reveals that the oldest brother is both married and the tallest. By statement 3, John cannot be the tallest. Since John is not the tallest, he is not the oldest. Thus, the oldest brother must be Gary. The conclusion is proved.

23) (B) By statements 3 and 4, General Woundwort must have given the order to advance. Statement 2 then tells us that Brigade X will advance to the demilitarized zone, but not soon enough before the conflict begins. Thus, the conclusion is disproved.

24) (A) If the distance is 5 miles or less, then the cost for the Orange Cab is only $7.50, whereas the cost for the Chubby Cab is $5 + 3x, where x represents the number of miles traveled. For 1 to 5 miles, the cost of the Chubby Cab is between $8 and $20. This means that for a distance of 5 miles, the Orange Cab costs $7.50, whereas the Chubby Cab costs $20. After 5 miles, the cost per mile of the Chubby Cab exceeds the cost per mile of the Orange Cab. Thus, regardless of the actual distance between Fullerton and Elverton, the cost for the Orange Cab will be cheaper than that of the Chubby Cab.

25) (B) It looks like "Dalton" should be replaced by "Dan in the conclusion. Then by statement 1, if Lucy is absent, Dan is never in class. Thus, the conclusion is disproved.

READING COMPREHENSION
UNDERSTANDING AND INTERPRETING WRITTEN MATERIAL

EXAMINATION SECTION
TEST 1

DIRECTIONS: Each question or incomplete statement is followed by several suggested answers or completions. Select the one that BEST answers the question or completes the statement. *PRINT THE LETTER OF THE CORRECT ANSWER IN THE SPACE AT THE RIGHT.*

Questions 1-5.

DIRECTIONS: Questions 1 through 5 are to be answered on the basis of the following passage.

The laws with which criminal courts are concerned contain threats of punishment for infraction of specified rules. Consequently, the courts are organized primarily for implementation of the punitive societal reaction of crime. While the informal organization of most courts allows the judge to use discretion as to which guilty persons actually are to be punished, the threat of punishment for all guilty persons always is present. Also, in recent years a number of formal provisions for the use of non-punitive and treatment methods by the criminal courts have been made, but the threat of punishment remains, even for the recipients of the treatment and non-punitive measures. For example, it has become possible for courts to grant probation, which can be non-punitive, to some offenders, but the probationer is constantly under the threat of punishment, for, if he does not maintain the conditions of his probation, he may be imprisoned. As the treatment reaction to crime becomes more popular, the criminal courts may have as their sole function the determination of the guilt or innocence of the accused persons, leaving the problem of correcting criminals entirely to outsiders. Under such conditions, the organization of the court system, the duties and activities of court personnel, and the nature of the trial all would be decidedly different.

1. Which one of the following is the BEST description of the subject matter of the above passage?
   The

   A. value of non-punitive measures for criminals
   B. effect of punishment on guilty individuals
   C. punitive functions of the criminal courts
   D. success of probation as a deterrent of crime

   1.____

2. It may be INFERRED from the above passage that the present traditional organization of the criminal court system is a result of

   A. the nature of the laws with which these courts are concerned
   B. a shift from non-punitive to punitive measures for correctional purposes
   C. an informal arrangement between court personnel and the government
   D. a formal decision made by court personnel to increase efficiency

   2.____

3. All persons guilty of breaking certain specified rules, according to the above passage, are subject to the threat of   3.____

    A. treatment   B. punishment
    C. probation   D. retrial

4. According to the above passage, the decision whether or not to punish a guilty person is a function USUALLY performed by   4.____

    A. the jury   B. the criminal code
    C. the judge   D. corrections personnel

5. According to the above passage, which one of the following is a possible effect of an increase in the *treatment reactions to crime?*   5.____

    A. A decrease in the number of court personnel
    B. An increase in the number of criminal trials
    C. Less reliance on probation as a non-punitive treatment measure
    D. A decrease in the functions of the court following determination of guilt

Questions 6-8.

DIRECTIONS: Questions 6 through 8 are to be answered on the basis of the following passage.

A glaring exception to the usual practice of the judicial trial as a means of conflict resolution is the utilization of administrative hearings. The growing tendency to create administrative bodies with rule-making and quasi-judicial powers has shattered many standard concepts. A comprehensive examination of the legal process cannot neglect these newer patterns.

In the administrative process, the legislative, executive, and judicial functions are mixed together, and many functions, such as investigating, advocating, negotiating, testifying, rule making, and adjudicating, are carried out by the same agency. The reason for the breakdown of the separation-of-powers formula is not hard to find. It was felt by Congress, and state and municipal legislatures, that certain regulatory tasks could not be performed efficiently, rapidly, expertly, and with due concern for the public interest by the traditional branches of government. Accordingly, regulatory agencies were delegated powers to consider disputes from the earliest stage of investigation to the final stages of adjudication entirely within each agency itself, subject only to limited review in the regular courts.

6. The above passage states that the usual means for conflict resolution is through the use of   6.____

    A. judicial trial   B. administrative hearing
    C. legislation   D. regulatory agencies

7. The above passage IMPLIES that the use of administrative hearing in resolving conflict is a(n) _____ approach.   7.____

    A. traditional   B. new
    C. dangerous   D. experimental

8. The above passage states that the reason for the breakdown of the separation-of-powers formula in the administrative process is that   8.____

A. Congress believed that certain regulatory tasks could be better performed by separate agencies
B. legislative and executive functions are incompatible in the same agency
C. investigative and regulatory functions are not normally reviewed by the courts
D. state and municipal legislatures are more concerned with efficiency than with legality

Questions 9-10.

DIRECTIONS: Questions 9 and 10 are to be answered SOLELY on the basis of the information given in the following paragraph.

An assumption commonly made in regard to the reliability of testimony is that when a number of persons report upon the same matter, those details upon which there is an agreement may, in general, be considered as substantiated. Experiments have shown, however, that there is a tendency for the same errors to appear in the testimony of different individuals, and that, quite apart from any collusion, agreement of testimony is no proof of dependability.

9. According to the above paragraph, it is commonly assumed that details of an event are substantiated when   9._____

A. a number of persons report upon them
B. a reliable person testifies to them
C. no errors are apparent in the testimony of different individuals
D. several witnesses are in agreement about them

10. According to the above paragraph, agreement in the testimony of different witnesses to the same event is   10._____

A. evaluated more reliably when considered apart from collusion
B. not the result of chance
C. not a guarantee of the accuracy of the facts
D. the result of a mass reaction of the witnesses

Questions 11-12.

DIRECTIONS: Questions 11 and 12 are to be answered SOLELY on the basis of the information given in the following paragraph.

The accuracy of the information about past occurrence obtainable in an interview is so low that one must take the stand that the best use to be made of the interview in this connection is a means of finding clues and avenues of access to more reliable sources of information. On the other hand, feelings and attitudes have been found to be clearly and correctly revealed in a properly conducted personal interview.

11. According to the above paragraph, information obtained in a personal interview   11._____

A. can be corroborated by other clues and more reliable sources of information revealed at the interview
B. can be used to develop leads to other sources of information about past events
C. is not reliable
D. is reliable if it relates to recent occurrences

12. According to the above paragraph, the personal interview is suitable for obtaining   12.____

    A. emotional reactions to a given situation
    B. fresh information on factors which may be forgotten
    C. revived recollection of previous events for later use as testimony
    D. specific information on material already reduced to writing

Questions 13-15.

DIRECTIONS: Questions 13 through 15 are to be answered on the basis of the following paragraph.

Admissibility of handwriting standards (samples of handwriting for the purpose of comparison) as a basis for expert testimony is frequently necessary when the authenticity of disputed documents may be at issue. Under the older rules of common law, only that writing relating to the issues in the case could be used as a basis for handwriting testimony by an expert. Today, most jurisdictions admit irrelevant writings as standards for comparison. However, their genuineness, in all instances, must be established to the satisfaction of the court. There are a number of types of documents, however, not ordinarily relevant to the issues which are seldom acceptable to the court as handwriting standards, such as bail bonds, signatures on affidavits, depositions, etc. These are usually already before the court as part of the record in a case. Exhibits written in the presence of a witness or prepared voluntarily for a law enforcement officer are readily admissible in most jurisdictions. Testimony of a witness who is considered familiar with the writing is admissible in some jurisdictions. In criminal cases, it is possible that the signature on the fingerprint card obtained in connection with the arrest of the defendant for the crime currently charged may be admitted as a handwriting standard. In order to give the defendant the fairest possible treatment, most jurisdictions do not admit the signatures on fingerprint cards pertaining to prior arrests. However, they are admitted sometimes. In such instances, the court usually requires that the signature be photographed or removed from the card and no reference be made to the origin of the signature.

13. Of the following, the types of handwriting standards MOST likely to be admitted in evidence by most jurisdictions are those   13.____

    A. appearing on depositions and bail bonds
    B. which were written in the presence of a witness or voluntarily given to a law enforcement officer
    C. identified by witnesses who claim to be familiar with the handwriting
    D. which are in conformity with the rules of common law only

14. The PRINCIPAL factor which generally determines the acceptance of handwriting standards by the courts is   14.____

    A. the relevance of the submitted documents to the issues of the case
    B. the number of witnesses who have knowledge of the submitted documents
    C. testimony that the writing has been examined by a handwriting expert
    D. acknowledgment by the court of the authenticity of the submitted documents

15. The MOST logical reason for requiring the removal of the signature of a defendant from fingerprint cards pertaining to prior arrests, before admitting the signature in court as a handwriting standard, is that   15.____

A. it simplifies the process of identification of the signature as a standard for comparison
B. the need for identifying the fingerprints is eliminated
C. mention of prior arrests may be prejudicial to the defendant
D. a handwriting expert does not need information pertaining to prior arrests in order to make his identification

Questions 16-20.

DIRECTIONS: Questions 16 through 20 are to be answered SOLELY on the basis of the information contained in the following paragraph.

A statement which is offered in an attempt to prove the truth of the matters therein stated, but which is not made by the author as a witness before the court at the particular trial in which it is so offered, is hearsay. This is so whether the statement consists of words (oral or written), of symbols used as a substitute for words, or of signs or other conduct offered as the equivalent of a statement. Subject to some well-established exceptions, hearsay is not generally acceptable as evidence, and it does not become competent evidence just because it is received by the court without objection. One basis for this rule is simply that a fact cannot be proved by showing that somebody stated it was a fact. Another basis for the rule is the fundamental principle that in a criminal prosecution the testimony of the witness shall be taken before the court, so that at the time he gives the testimony offered in evidence he will be sworn and subject to cross-examination, the scrutiny of the court, and confrontation by the accused.

16. Which of the following is hearsay?   16.____
    A(n)

    A. written statement by a person not present at the court hearing where the statement is submitted as proof of an occurrence
    B. oral statement in court by a witness of what he saw
    C. written statement of what he saw by a witness present in court
    D. re-enactment by a witness in court of what he saw

17. In a criminal case, a statement by a person not present in court is   17.____

    A. *acceptable* evidence if not objected to by the prosecutor
    B. *acceptable* evidence if not objected to by the defense lawyer
    C. *not acceptable* evidence except in certain well-settled circumstances
    D. *not acceptable* evidence under any circumstances

18. The rule on hearsay is founded on the belief that   18.____

    A. proving someone said an act occurred is not proof that the act did occur
    B. a person who has knowledge about a case should be willing to appear in court
    C. persons not present in court are likely to be unreliable witnesses
    D. permitting persons to testify without appearing in court will lead to a disrespect for law

19. One reason for the general rule that a witness in a criminal case must give his testimony   19.____
    in court is that

    A. a witness may be influenced by threats to make untrue statements
    B. the opposite side is then permitted to question him
    C. the court provides protection for a witness against unfair questioning
    D. the adversary system is designed to prevent a miscarriage of justice

20. Of the following, the MOST appropriate title for the above passage would be   20.____

    A. WHAT IS HEARSAY?   B. RIGHTS OF DEFENDANTS
    C. TRIAL PROCEDURES   D. TESTIMONY OF WITNESSES

21. A person's statements are independent of who he is or what he is. Statements made by   21.____
    a person are not proved true or false by questioning his character or his position. A state-
    ment should stand or fall on its merits, regardless of who makes the statement. Truth is
    determined by evidence only. A person's character or personality should not be the
    determining factor in logic.   Discussions should not become incidents of name calling.
    According to the above, whether or not a statement is true depends on the

    A. recipient's conception of validity
    B. maker's reliability
    C. extent of support by facts
    D. degree of merit the discussion has

Question 22-25.

DIRECTIONS: Questions 22 through 25 are to be answered on the basis of the following pas-
               sage.

    The question, whether an act, repugnant to the Constitution, can become the law of the
land, is a question deeply interesting to the United States; but, happily, not of an intricacy pro-
portioned to its interest. It seems only necessary to recognize certain principles, supposed to
have been long and well-established, to decide it. That the people have an original right to
establish, for their future government, such principles as, in their opinion, shall most conduce
to their own happiness, is the basis on which the whole American fabric has been erected.
The exercise of this original right is a very great exertion; nor can it, nor ought it, to be frequently repeated. The principles, therefore, so established are deemed fundamental; and as
the authority from which they proceed is supreme, and can seldom act, they are designed to
be permanent.

22. The BEST title for the above passage would be   22.____

    A. PRINCIPLES OF THE CONSTITUTION
    B. THE ROOT OF CONSTITUTIONAL CHANGE
    C. ONLY PEOPLE CAN CHANGE THE CONSTITUTION
    D. METHODS OF CONSTITUTIONAL CHANGE

23. According to the above passage, original right is   23.____

    A. fundamental to the principle that the people may choose their own form of govern-
        ment
    B. established by the Constitution

C. the result of a very great exertion and should not often be repeated

D. supreme, can seldom act, and is designed to be permanent

24. Whether an act not in keeping with Constitutional principles can become law is, according to the above passage, 24.____

    A. an intricate problem requiring great thought and concentration

    B. determined by the proportionate interests of legislators

    C. determined by certain long established principles, fundamental to Constitutional Law

    D. an intricate problem, but less intricate than it would seem from the interest shown in it

25. According to the above passage, the phrase *and can seldom act* refers to the 25.____

    A. principle enacted early into law by Americans when they chose their future form of government

    B. original rights of the people as vested in the Constitution

    C. original framers of the Constitution

    D. established, fundamental principles of government

_____

KEY (CORRECT ANSWERS)

1. C		11. B	
2. A		12. A	
3. B		13. B	
4. C		14. D	
5. D		15. C	
6. A		16. A	
7. B		17. C	
8. A		18. A	
9. D		19. B	
10. C		20. A	

21.	C
22.	B
23.	A
24.	D
25.	A

_____

TEST 2

DIRECTIONS: Each question or incomplete statement is followed by several suggested answers or completions. Select the one that BEST answers the question or completes the statement. *PRINT THE LETTER OF THE CORRECT ANSWER IN THE SPACE AT THE RIGHT.*

Questions 1-3.

DIRECTIONS: Questions 1 through 3 are to be answered SOLELY on the basis of the following paragraph.

The police laboratory performs a valuable service in crime investigation by assisting in the reconstruction of criminal action and by aiding in the identification of persons and things. When studied by a technician, physical things found at crime scenes often reveal facts useful in identifying the criminal and in determining what has occurred. The nature of substances to be examined and the character of the examination to be made vary so widely that the services of a large variety of skilled scientific persons are needed in crime investigations. To employ such a complete staff and to provide them with equipment and standards needed for all possible analysis and comparisons is beyond the means and the needs of any but the largest police departments. The search of crime scenes for physical evidence also calls for the services of specialists supplied with essential equipment and assigned to each tour of duty so as to provide service at any hour.

1. If a police department employs a large staff of technicians of various types in its laboratory, it will affect crime investigations to the extent that   1._____

   A. most crimes will be speedily solved
   B. identification of criminals will be aided
   C. search of crime scenes for physical evidence will become of less importance
   D. investigation by police officers will not usually be required

2. According to the above paragraph, the MOST complete study of objects found at the scenes of crimes is   2._____

   A. always done in all large police departments
   B. based on assigning one technician to each tour of duty
   C. probably done only in large police departments
   D. probably done in police departments of communities with low crime rates

3. According to the above paragraph, a large variety of skilled technicians is useful in criminal investigations because   3._____

   A. crimes cannot be solved without their assistance as part of the police team
   B. large police departments need large staffs
   C. many different kinds of tests on various substances can be made
   D. the police cannot predict what methods may be tried by wily criminals

Questions 4-6.

DIRECTIONS: Questions 4 through 6 are to be answered SOLELY on the basis of the following passage.

Probably the most important single mechanism for bringing the resources of science and technology to bear on the problems of crime would be the establishment of a major prestigious science and technology research program within a research institute. The program would create interdisciplinary teams of mathematicians, computer scientists, electronics engineers, physicists, biologists, and other natural scientists, psychologists, sociologists, economists, and lawyers. The institute and the program must be significant enough to attract the best scientists available, and, to this end, the director of this institute must himself have a background in science and technology and have the respect of scientists. Because it would be difficult to attract such a staff into the Federal government, the institute should be established by a university, a group of universities, or an independent nonprofit organization, and should be within a major metropolitan area. The institute would have to establish close ties with neighboring criminal justice agencies that would receive the benefit of serving as experimental laboratories for such an institute. In fact, the proposal for the institute might be jointly submitted with the criminal justice agencies. The research program would require, in order to bring together the necessary *critical mass* of competent staff, an annual budget which might reach 5 million dollars, funded with at least three years of lead time to assure continuity. Such a major scientific and technological research institute should be supported by the Federal government.

4. Of the following, the MOST appropriate title for the foregoing passage is   4.____

   A. RESEARCH - AN INTERDISCIPLINARY APPROACH TO FIGHTING CRIME
   B. A CURRICULUM FOR FIGHTING CRIME
   C. THE ROLE OF THE UNIVERSITY IN THE FIGHT AGAINST CRIME
   D. GOVERNMENTAL SUPPORT OF CRIMINAL RESEARCH PROGRAMS

5. According to the above passage, in order to attract the best scientists available, the   5.____
   research institute should

   A. provide psychologists and sociologists to counsel individual members of interdisciplinary teams
   B. encourage close ties with neighboring criminal justice agencies
   C. be led by a person who is respected in the scientific community
   D. be directly operated and funded by the Federal government

6. The term *critical mass,* as used in the above passage, refers MAINLY to   6.____

   A. a staff which would remain for three years of continuous service to the institute
   B. staff members necessary to carry out the research program of the institute successfully
   C. the staff necessary to establish relations with criminal justice agencies which will serve as experimental laboratories for the institute
   D. a staff which would be able to assist the institute in raising adequate funds

Questions 7-9.

DIRECTIONS: Questions 7 through 9 are to be answered SOLELY on the basis of the following paragraph.

The use of modern scientific methods in the examination of physical evidence often provides information to the investigator which he could not otherwise obtain. This applies particularly to small objects and materials present in minute quantities or trace evidence because the quantities here are such that they may be overlooked without methodical searching, and often special means of detection are needed. Whenever two objects come in contact with one another, there is a transfer of material, however slight. Usually, the softer object will transfer to the harder, but the transfer may be mutual. The quantity of material transferred differs with the type of material involved and the more violent the contact the greater the degree of transference. Through scientific methods of determining physical properties and chemical composition, we can add to the facts observable by the investigator's unaided senses, and thereby increase the chances of identification.

7. According to the above paragraph, the amount of material transferred whenever two objects come in contact with one another

    A. varies directly with the softness of the objects involved
    B. varies directly with the violence of the contact of the objects
    C. is greater when two soft, rather than hard, objects come into violent contact with each other
    D. is greater when coarse-grained, rather than smooth-grained, materials are involved

7.____

8. According to the above paragraph, the PRINCIPAL reason for employing scientific methods in obtaining trace evidence is that

    A. other methods do not involve a methodical search of the crime scene
    B. scientific methods of examination frequently reveal physical evidence which did not previously exist
    C. the amount of trace evidence may be so sparse that other methods are useless
    D. trace evidence cannot be properly identified unless special means of detection are employed

8.____

9. According to the above paragraph, the one of the following statements which BEST describes the manner in which scientific methods of analyzing physical evidence assists the investigator is that such methods

    A. add additional valuable information to the investigator's own knowledge of complex and rarely occurring materials found as evidence
    B. compensate for the lack of important evidential material through the use of physical and chemical analyses
    C. make possible an analysis of evidence which goes beyond the ordinary capacity of the investigator's senses
    D. identify precisely those physical characteristics of the individual which the untrained senses of the investigator are unable to discern

9.____

Questions 10-13.

DIRECTIONS: Questions 10 through 13 are to be answered SOLELY on the basis of the information contained in the following paragraph.

Under the provisions of the Bank Protection Act of 1968, enacted July 8, 1968, each Federal banking supervisory agency, as of January 7, 1969, had to issue rules establishing minimum standards with which financial institutions under their control must comply with respect to the installation, maintenance, and operation of security devices and procedures, reasonable in cost, to discourage robberies, burglaries, and larcenies, and to assist in the identification and apprehension of persons who commit such acts. The rules set the time limits within which the affected banks and savings and loan associations must comply with the standards, and the rules require the submission of periodic reports on the steps taken. A violator of a rule under this Act is subject to a civil penalty not to exceed $100 for each day of the violation. The enforcement of these regulations rests with the responsible banking supervisory agencies.

10. The Bank Protection Act of 1968 was designed to
10.____

    A. provide Federal police protection for banks covered by the Act
    B. have organizations covered by the Act take precautions against criminals
    C. set up a system for reporting all bank robberies to the FBI
    D. insure institutions covered by the Act from financial loss due to robberies, burglaries, and larcenies

11. Under the provisions of the Bank Protection Act of 1968, each Federal banking supervisory agency was required to set up rules for financial institutions covered by the Act governing the
11.____

    A. hiring of personnel
    B. punishment of burglars
    C. taking of protective measures
    D. penalties for violations

12. Financial institutions covered by the Bank Protection Act of 1968 were required to
12.____

    A. file reports at regular intervals on what they had done to prevent theft
    B. identify and apprehend persons who commit robberies, burglaries, and larcenies
    C. draw up a code of ethics for their employees
    D. have fingerprints of their employees filed with the FBI

13. Under the provisions of the Bank Protection Act of 1968, a bank which is subject to the rules established under the Act and which violates a rule is liable to a penalty of NOT _____ than $100 for each _____.
13.____

    A. more; violation   B. less; day of violation
    C. less; violation   D. more; day of violation

Questions 14-17.

DIRECTIONS: Questions 14 through 17 are to be answered SOLELY on the basis of the following passage.

Specific measures for prevention of pilferage will be based on careful analysis of the conditions at each agency. The most practical and effective method to control casual pilferage is the establishment of psychological deterrents.

One of the most common means of discouraging casual pilferage is to search individuals leaving the agency at unannounced times and places. These spot searches may occasionally detect attempts at theft, but greater value is realized by bringing to the attention of individuals the fact that they may be apprehended if they do attempt the illegal removal of property.

An aggressive security education program is an effective means of convincing employees that they have much more to lose than they do to gain by engaging in acts of theft. It is important for all employees to realize that pilferage is morally wrong no matter how insignificant the value of the item which is taken. In establishing any deterrent to casual pilferage, security officers must not lose sight of the fact that most employees are honest and disapprove of thievery. Mutual respect between security personnel and other employees of the agency must be maintained if the facility is to be protected from other more dangerous forms of human hazards. Any security measure which infringes on the human rights or dignity of others will jeopardize, rather than enhance, the overall protection of the agency.

14. The $100,000 yearly inventory of an agency revealed that $50 worth of goods had been stolen; the only individuals with access to the stolen materials were the employees. Of the following measures, which would the author of the above passage MOST likely recommend to a security officer?

    A. Conduct an intensive investigation of all employees to find the culprit.
    B. Make a record of the theft, but take no investigative or disciplinary action against any employee.
    C. Place a tight security check on all future movements of personnel.
    D. Remove the remainder of the material to an area with much greater security.

14.____

15. What does the passage imply is the percentage of employees whom a security officer should expect to be honest?

    A. No employee can be expected to be honest all of the time
    B. Just 50%
    C. Less than 50%
    D. More than 50%

15.____

16. According to the above passage, the security officer would use which of the following methods to minimize theft in buildings with many exits when his staff is very small?

    A. Conduct an inventory of all material and place a guard near that which is most likely to be pilfered
    B. Inform employees of the consequences of legal prosecution for pilfering
    C. Close off the unimportant exits and have all his men concentrate on a few exits
    D. Place a guard at each exit and conduct a casual search of individuals leaving the premises

16.____

17. Of the following, the title BEST suited for this passage is

    A. CONTROL MEASURES FOR CASUAL PILFERING
    B. DETECTING THE POTENTIAL PILFERER
    C. FINANCIAL LOSSES RESULTING FROM PILFERING
    D. THE USE OF MORAL PERSUASION IN PHYSICAL SECURITY

17.____

Questions 18-24.

DIRECTIONS: Questions 18 through 24 are to be answered SOLELY on the basis of the following passage.

Burglar alarms are designed to detect intrusion automatically. Robbery alarms enable a victim of a robbery or an attack to signal for help. Such devices can be located in elevators, hallways, homes and apartments, businesses and factories, and subways, as well as on the street in high-crime areas. Alarms could deter some potential criminals from attacking targets so protected. If alarms were prevalent and not visible, then they might serve to suppress crime generally. In addition, of course, the alarms can summon the police when they are needed.

All alarms must perform three functions: sensing or initiation of the signal, transmission of the signal and annunciation of the alarm. A burglar alarm needs a sensor to detect human presence or activity in an unoccupied enclosed area like a building or a room. A robbery victim would initiate the alarm by closing a foot or wall switch, or by triggering a portable transmitter which would send the alarm signal to a remote receiver. The signal can sound locally as a loud noise to frighten away a criminal, or it can be sent silently by wire to a central agency. A centralized annunciator requires either private lines from each alarmed point, or the transmission of some information on the location of the signal.

18. A conclusion which follows LOGICALLY from the above passage is that 18.____

    A. burglar alarms employ sensor devices; robbery alarms make use of initiation devices
    B. robbery alarms signal intrusion without the help of the victim; burglar alarms require the victim to trigger a switch
    C. robbery alarms sound locally; burglar alarms are transmitted to a central agency
    D. the mechanisms for a burglar alarm and a robbery alarm are alike

19. According to the above passage, alarms can be located 19.____

    A. in a wide variety of settings
    B. only in enclosed areas
    C. at low cost in high-crime areas
    D. only in places where potential criminals will be deterred

20. According to the above passage, which of the following is ESSENTIAL if a signal is to be received in a central office? 20.____

    A. A foot or wall switch
    B. A noise-producing mechanism
    C. A portable reception device
    D. Information regarding the location of the source

21. According to the above passage, an alarm system can function WITHOUT a 21.____

    A. centralized annunciating device
    B. device to stop the alarm
    C. sensing or initiating device
    D. transmission device

22. According to the above passage, the purpose of robbery alarms is to 22.____

    A. find out automatically whether a robbery has taken place
    B. lower the crime rate in high-crime areas
    C. make a loud noise to frighten away the criminal
    D. provide a victim with the means to signal for help

23. According to the above passage, alarms might aid in lessening crime if they were   23._____

    A. answered promptly by police
    B. completely automatic
    C. easily accessible to victims
    D. hidden and widespread

24. Of the following, the BEST title for the above passage is   24._____

    A. DETECTION OF CRIME BY ALARMS
    B. LOWERING THE CRIME RATE
    C. SUPPRESSION OF CRIME
    D. THE PREVENTION OF ROBBERY

25. Although the rural crime reporting area is much less developed than that for cities and   25._____
    towns, current data are collected in sufficient volume to justify the generalization that
    rural crime rates are lower than those or urban communities.
    According to this statement,

    A. better reporting of crime occurs in rural areas than in cities
    B. there appears to be a lower proportion of crime in rural areas than in cities
    C. cities have more crime than towns
    D. crime depends on the amount of reporting

_____

KEY (CORRECT ANSWERS)

1.	B		11.	C
2.	C		12.	A
3.	C		13.	D
4.	A		14.	B
5.	C		15.	D
6.	B		16.	B
7.	B		17.	A
8.	C		18.	A
9.	C		19.	A
10.	B		20.	D

21.	A
22.	D
23.	D
24.	A
25.	B

_____

CLERICAL ABILITIES

EXAMINATION SECTION
TEST 1

DIRECTIONS: Each question or incomplete statement is followed by several suggested answers or completions. Select the one that BEST answers the question or completes the statement. *PRINT THE LETTER OF THE CORRECT ANSWER IN THE SPACE AT THE RIGHT.*

Questions 1-4.

DIRECTIONS: Questions 1 through 4 are to be answered on the basis of the information given below.

The most commonly used filing system and the one that is easiest to learn is alphabetical filing. This involves putting records in an A to Z order, according to the letters of the alphabet. The name of a person is filed by using the following order: first, the surname or last name; second, the first name; third, the middle name or middle initial. For example, *Henry C. Young* is filed under *Y* and thereafter under *Young, Henry C.* The name of a company is filed in the same way. For example, *Long Cabinet Co.* is filed under *L*, while *John T. Long Cabinet Co.* is filed under *L* and thereafter under *Long., John T. Cabinet Co.*

1. The one of the following which lists the names of persons in the CORRECT alphabetical order is:

    A. Mary Carrie, Helen Carrol, James Carson, John Carter
    B. James Carson, Mary Carrie, John Carter, Helen Carrol
    C. Helen Carrol, James Carson, John Carter, Mary Carrie
    D. John Carter, Helen Carrol, Mary Carrie, James Carson

1.____

2. The one of the following which lists the names of persons in the CORRECT alphabetical order is:

    A. Jones, John C.; Jones, John A.; Jones, John P.; Jones, John K.
    B. Jones, John P.; Jones, John K.; Jones, John C.; Jones, John A.
    C. Jones, John A.; Jones, John C.; Jones, John K.; Jones, John P.
    D. Jones, John K.; Jones, John C.; Jones, John A.; Jones, John P.

2.____

3. The one of the following which lists the names of the companies in the CORRECT alphabetical order is:

    A. Blane Co., Blake Co., Block Co., Blear Co.
    B. Blake Co., Blane Co., Blear Co., Block Co.
    C. Block Co., Blear Co., Blane Co., Blake Co.
    D. Blear Co., Blake Co., Blane Co., Block Co.

3.____

4. You are to return to the file an index card on *Barry C. Wayne Materials and Supplies Co.* Of the following, the CORRECT alphabetical group that you should return the index card to is

    A. A to G   B. H to M   C. N to S   D. T to Z

4.____

Questions 5-10.

DIRECTIONS: In each of Questions 5 through 10, the names of four people are given. For each question, choose as your answer the one of the four names given which should be filed FIRST according to the usual system of alphabetical filing of names, as described in the following paragraph.

In filing names, you must start with the last name. Names are filed in order of the first letter of the last name, then the second letter, etc. Therefore, BAILY would be filed before BROWN, which would be filed before COLT. A name with fewer letters of the same type comes first; i.e., Smith before Smithe. If the last names are the same, the names are filed alphabetically by the first name. If the first name is an initial, a name with an initial would come before a first name that starts with the same letter as the initial. Therefore, I. BROWN would come before IRA BROWN. Finally, if both last name and first name are the same, the name would be filed alphabetically by the middle name, once again an initial coming before a middle name which starts with the same letter as the initial. If there is no middle name at all, the name would come before those with middle initials or names.

Sample Question: A.   Lester Daniels
        B.   William Dancer
        C.   Nathan Danzig
        D.   Dan Lester

The last names beginning with D are filed before the last name beginning with L. Since DANIELS, DANCER, and DANZIG all begin with the same three letters, you must look at the fourth letter of the last name to determine which name should be filed first. C comes before I or Z in the alphabet, so DANCER is filed before DANIELS or DANZIG. Therefore, the answer to the above sample question is B.

5. A.   Scott Biala
  B.   Mary Byala
  C.   Martin Baylor
  D.   Francis Bauer

5._____

6. A.   Howard J. Black
  B.   Howard Black
  C.   J. Howard Black
  D.   John H. Black

6._____

7. A.   Theodora Garth Kingston
  B.   Theadore Barth Kingston
  C.   Thomas Kingston
  D.   Thomas T. Kingston

7._____

8. A.   Paulette Mary Huerta
  B.   Paul M. Huerta
  C.   Paulette L. Huerta
  D.   Peter A. Huerta

8._____

9. A. Martha Hunt Morgan
    B. Martin Hunt Morgan
    C. Mary H. Morgan
    D. Martine H. Morgan

9._____

10. A. James T. Meerschaum
    B. James M. Mershum
    C. James F. Mearshaum
    D. James N. Meshum

10._____

Questions 11-14.

DIRECTIONS: Questions 11 through 14 are to be answered SOLELY on the basis of the following information.

You are required to file various documents in file drawers which are labeled according to
the following pattern:

DOCUMENTS

MEMOS		LETTERS	
File	Subject	File	Subject
84PM1 -	(A-L)	84PC1 -	(A-L)
84PM2 -	(M-Z)	84PC2 -	(M-Z)

REPORTS		INQUIRIES	
File Subject		File	Subject
84PR1 -	(A-L)	84PQ1 -	(A-L)
84PR2 -	(M-Z)	84PQ2 -	(M-Z)

11. A letter dealing with a burglary should be filed in the drawer labeled

    A. 84PM1   B. 84PC1   C. 84PR1   D. 84PQ2

11._____

12. A report on Statistics should be found in the drawer labeled

    A. 84PM1   B. 84PC2   C. 84PR2   D. 84PQ2

12._____

13. An inquiry is received about parade permit procedures. It should be filed in the drawer
    labeled

    A. 84PM2   B. 84PC1   C. 84PR1   D. 84PQ2

13._____

14. A police officer has a question about a robbery report you filed.
    You should pull this file from the drawer labeled

    A. 84PM1   B. 84PM2   C. 84PR1   D. 84PR2

14._____

Questions 15-22.

DIRECTIONS: Each of Questions 15 through 22 consists of four or six numbered names. For
each question, choose the option (A, B, C, or D) which indicates the order in
which the names should be filed in accordance with the following filing instructions:
- File alphabetically according to last name, then first name, then middle initial.
- File according to each successive letter within a name.

- When comparing two names in which, the letters in the longer name are identical to the corresponding letters in the shorter name, the shorter name is filed first.
- When the last names are the same, initials are always filed before names beginning with the same letter.

15.
    I.   Ralph Robinson
    II.   Alfred Ross
    III.   Luis Robles
    IV.   James Roberts
The CORRECT filing sequence for the above names should be

    A. IV, II, I, III
    C. III, IV, I, II
                  B. I, IV, III, II
                  D. IV, I, III, II

15.____

16.
    I.   Irwin Goodwin
    II.   Inez Gonzalez
    III.   Irene Goodman
    IV.   Ira S. Goodwin
    V.   Ruth I. Goldstein
    VI.   M.B. Goodman
The CORRECT filing sequence for the above names should be

    A. V, II, I, IV, III, VI
    C. V, II, III, VI, IV, I
                  B. V, II, VI, III, IV, I
                  D. V, II, III, VI, I, IV

16.____

17.
    I.   George Allan
    II.   Gregory Allen
    III.   Gary Allen
    IV.   George Allen
The CORRECT filing sequence for the above names should be

    A. IV, III, I, II
    C. III, IV, I, II
                  B. I, IV, II, III
                  D. I, III, IV, II

17.____

18.
    I.   Simon Kauffman
    II.   Leo Kaufman
    III.   Robert Kaufmann
    IV.   Paul Kauffmann
The CORRECT filing sequence for the above names should be

    A. I, IV, II, III
    C. III, II, IV, I
                  B. II, IV, III, I
                  D. I, II, III, IV

18.____

19.
    I.   Roberta Williams
    II.   Robin Wilson
    III.   Roberta Wilson
    IV.   Robin Williams
The CORRECT filing sequence for the above names should be

    A. III, II, IV, I
    C. I, II, III, IV
                  B. I, IV, III, II
                  D. III, I, II, IV

19.____

20.
    I.   Lawrence Shultz
    II.   Albert Schultz
    III. Theodore Schwartz
    IV. Thomas Schwarz
    V.   Alvin Schultz
    VI. Leonard Shultz

The CORRECT filing sequence for the above names should be

20.____

  A. II, V, III, IV, I, VI   B. IV, III, V, I, II, VI
  C. II, V, I, VI, III, IV   D. I, VI, II, V, III, IV

21.
    I.   McArdle
    II.   Mayer
    III. Maletz
    IV. McNiff
    V.   Meyer
    VI. MacMahon

The CORRECT filing sequence for the above names should be

21.____

  A. I, IV, VI, III, II, V   B. II, I, IV, VI, III, V
  C. VI, III, II, I, IV, V   D. VI, III, II, V, I, IV

22.
    I.   Jack E. Johnson
    II.   R.H. Jackson
    III. Bertha Jackson
    IV. J.T. Johnson
    V.   Ann Johns
    VI. John Jacobs

The CORRECT filing sequence for the above names should be

22.____

  A. II, III, VI, V, IV, I   B. III, II, VI, V, IV, I
  C. VI, II, III, I, V, IV   D. III, II, VI, IV, V, I

Questions 23-30.

DIRECTIONS: The code table below shows 10 letters with matching numbers. For each question, there are three sets of letters. Each set of letters is followed by a set of numbers which may or may not match their correct letter according to the code table. For each question, check all three sets of letters and numbers and mark your answer:
    A. if no pairs are correctly matched
    B. if only one pair is correctly matched
    C. if only two pairs are correctly matched
    D. if all three pairs are correctly matched

CODE TABLE

T	M	V	D	S	P	R	G	B	H
1	2	3	4	5	6	7	8	9	0

Sample Question: TMVDSP - 123456
                      RGBHTM - 789011
                      DSPRGB - 256789

In the sample question above, the first set of numbers correctly matches its set of letters. But the second and third pairs contain mistakes. In the second pair, M is incorrectly matched with number 1. According to the code table, letter M should be correctly matched with number 2. In the third pair, the letter D is incorrectly matched with number 2. According to the code table, letter D should be correctly matched with number 4. Since only one of the pairs is correctly matched, the answer to this sample question is B.

23. RSBMRM 759262
     GDSRVH 845730
     VDBRTM 349713

23.____

24. TGVSDR 183247
     SMHRDP 520647
     TRMHSR 172057

24.____

25. DSPRGM 456782
     MVDBHT 234902
     HPMDBT 062491

25.____

26. BVPTRD 936184
     GDPHMB 807029
     GMRHMV 827032

26.____

27. MGVRSH 283750
     TRDMBS 174295
     SPRMGV 567283

27.____

28. SGBSDM 489542
     MGHPTM 290612
     MPBMHT 269301

28.____

29. TDPBHM 146902
     VPBMRS 369275
     GDMBHM 842902

29.____

30. MVPTBV 236194
     PDRTMB 647128
     BGTMSM 981232

30.____

KEY (CORRECT ANSWERS)

1.	A	11.	B	21.	C
2.	C	12.	C	22.	B
3.	B	13.	D	23.	B
4.	D	14.	D	24.	B
5.	D	15.	D	25.	C
6.	B	16.	C	26.	A
7.	B	17.	D	27.	D
8.	B	18.	A	28.	A
9.	A	19.	B	29.	D
10.	C	20.	A	30.	A

—————

TEST 2

DIRECTIONS: Each question or incomplete statement is followed by several suggested answers or completions. Select the one that BEST answers the question or completes the statement. *PRINT THE LETTER OF THE CORRECT ANSWER IN THE SPACE AT THE RIGHT.*

Questions 1-10.

DIRECTIONS: Questions 1 through 10 each consists of two columns, each containing four lines of names, numbers and/or addresses. For each question, compare the lines in Column I with the lines in Column II to see if they match exactly, and mark your answer A, B, C, or D, according to the following instructions:
- A. all four lines match exactly
- B. only three lines match exactly
- C. only two lines match exactly
- D. only one line matches exactly

	COLUMN I	COLUMN II	

1.
   I. Earl Hodgson   Earl Hodgson
   II. 1409870   1408970
   III. Shore Ave.   Schore Ave.
   IV. Macon Rd.   Macon Rd.   1._____

2.
   I. 9671485   9671485
   II. 470 Astor Court   470 Astor Court
   III. Halprin, Phillip   Halperin, Phillip
   IV. Frank D. Poliseo   Frank D. Poliseo   2._____

3.
   I. Tandem Associates   Tandom Associates
   II. 144-17 Northern Blvd. 144-17 Northern Blvd.
   III. Alberta Forchi   Albert Forchi
   IV. Kings Park, NY 10751 Kings Point, NY 10751 3._____

4.
   I. Bertha C. McCormack Bertha C. McCormack
   II. Clayton, MO.   Clayton, MO.
   III. 976-4242   976-4242
   IV. New City, NY 10951   New City, NY 10951 4._____

5.
   I. George C. Morill   George C. Morrill
   II. Columbia, SC 29201   Columbia, SD 29201
   III. Louis Ingham   Louis Ingham
   IV. 3406 Forest Ave.   3406 Forest Ave.   5._____

6.
   I. 506 S. Elliott Pl.   506 S. Elliott Pl.
   II. Herbert Hall   Hurbert Hall
   III. 4712 Rockaway Pkway 4712 Rockaway Pkway
   IV. 169 E. 7 St.   169 E. 7 St.   6._____

		COLUMN I	COLUMN II	
7.	I.	345 Park Ave.	345 Park Pl.	7.____
	II.	Colman Oven Corp.	Coleman Oven Corp.	
	III.	Robert Conte	Robert Conti	
	IV.	6179846	6179846	
8.	I.	Grigori Schierber	Grigori Schierber	8.____
	II.	Des Moines, Iowa	Des Moines, Iowa	
	III.	Gouverneur Hospital	Gouverneur Hospital	
	IV.	91-35 Cresskill Pl.	91-35 Cresskill Pl.	
9.	I.	Jeffery Janssen	Jeffrey Janssen	9.____
	II.	8041071	8041071	
	III.	40 Rockefeller Plaza	40 Rockafeller Plaza	
	IV.	407 6 St.	406 7 St.	
10.	I.	5971996	5871996	10.____
	II.	3113 Knickerbocker Ave.	3113 Knickerbocker Ave.	
	III.	8434 Boston Post Rd.	8424 Boston Post Rd.	
	IV.	Penn Station	Penn Station	

Questions 11-14.

DIRECTIONS: Questions 11 through 14 are to be answered by looking at the four groups of names and addresses listed below (I, II, III, and IV) and then finding out the number of groups that have their corresponding numbered lines exactly the same.

GROUP I
Line 1. Richmond General Hospital
Line 2. Geriatric Clinic
Line 3. 3975 Paerdegat St.
Line 4. Loudonville, New York 11538

GROUP II
Richman General Hospital
Geriatric Clinic
3975 Peardegat St.
Londonville, New York 11538

GROUP III
Line 1. Richmond General Hospital
Line 2. Geriatric Clinic
Line 3. 3795 Paerdegat St.
Line 4. Loudonville, New York 11358

GROUP IV
Richmend General Hospital
Geriatric Clinic
3975 Paerdegat St.
Loudonville, New York 11538

11. In how many groups is line one exactly the same?   11.____

    A. Two   B. Three   C. Four   D. None

12. In how many groups is line two exactly the same?   12.____

    A. Two   B. Three   C. Four   D. None

13. In how many groups is line three exactly the same?   13.____

    A. Two   B. Three   C. Four   D. None

14. In how many groups is line four exactly the same?   14.____

    A. Two   B. Three   C. Four   D. None

Questions 15-18.

DIRECTIONS: Each of Questions 15 through 18 has two lists of names and addresses. Each list contains three sets of names and addresses. Check each of the three sets in the list on the right to see if they are the same as the corresponding set in the list on the left. Mark your answers:
- A. if none of the sets in the right list are the same as those in the left list
- B. if only one of the sets in the right list is the same as those in the left list
- C. if only two of the sets in the right list are the same as those in the left list
- D. if all three sets in the right list are the same as those in the left list

15.   Mary T. Berlinger   Mary T. Berlinger   15.____
       2351 Hampton St.   2351 Hampton St.
       Monsey, N.Y. 20117   Monsey, N.Y. 20117

       Eduardo Benes   Eduardo Benes
       473 Kingston Avenue   473 Kingston Avenue
       Central Islip, N.Y. 11734   Central Islip, N.Y. 11734

       Alan Carrington Fuchs   Alan Carrington Fuchs
       17 Gnarled Hollow Road   17 Gnarled Hollow Road
       Los Angeles, CA 91635   Los Angeles, CA 91685

16.   David John Jacobson   David John Jacobson   16.____
       178 35 St. Apt. 4C   178 53 St. Apt. 4C
       New York, N.Y. 00927   New York, N.Y. 00927

       Ann-Marie Calonella   Ann-Marie Calonella
       7243 South Ridge Blvd.   7243 South Ridge Blvd.
       Bakersfield, CA 96714   Bakersfield, CA 96714

       Pauline M. Thompson   Pauline M. Thomson
       872 Linden Ave.   872 Linden Ave.
       Houston, Texas 70321   Houston, Texas 70321

17.   Chester LeRoy Masterton   Chester LeRoy Masterson   17.____
       152 Lacy Rd.   152 Lacy Rd.
       Kankakee, Ill. 54532   Kankakee, Ill. 54532

       William Maloney   William Maloney
       S. LaCrosse Pla.   S. LaCross Pla.
       Wausau, Wisconsin 52146   Wausau, Wisconsin 52146

       Cynthia V. Barnes   Cynthia V. Barnes
       16 Pines Rd.   16 Pines Rd.
       Greenpoint, Miss. 20376   Greenpoint, Miss. 20376

18.   Marcel Jean Frontenac   Marcel Jean Frontenac   18.____
             8 Burton On The Water   6 Burton On The Water
             Calender, Me. 01471   Calender, Me. 01471

             J. Scott Marsden   J. Scott Marsden
             174 S. Tipton St.   174 Tipton St.
             Cleveland, Ohio   Cleveland, Ohio

             Lawrence T. Haney   Lawrence T. Haney
             171 McDonough St.   171 McDonough St.
             Decatur, Ga. 31304   Decatur, Ga. 31304

Questions 19-26.

DIRECTIONS: Each of Questions 19 through 26 has two lists of numbers. Each list contains three sets of numbers. Check each of the three sets in the list on the right to see if they are the same as the corresponding set in the list on the left. Mark your answers:

        A.   if none of the sets in the right list are the same as those in the left list
        B.   if only one of the sets in the right list is the same as those in the left list
        C.   if only two of the sets in the right list are the same as those in the left list
        D.   if all three sets in the right list are the same as those in the left list

19.	7354183476	7354983476	19.____
	4474747744	4474747774	
	57914302311	57914302311	
20.	7143592185	7143892185	20.____
	8344517699	8344518699	
	9178531263	9178531263	
21.	2572114731	257214731	21.____
	8806835476	8806835476	
	8255831246	8255831246	
22.	331476853821	331476858621	22.____
	6976658532996	6976655832996	
	3766042113715	3766042113745	
23.	8806663315	8806663315	23.____
	74477138449	74477138449	
	211756663666	211756663666	
24.	990006966996	99000696996	24.____
	53022219743	53022219843	
	4171171117717	4171171177717	
25.	24400222433004	24400222433004	25.____
	5300030055000355	5300030055500355	
	20000075532002022	20000075532002022	

26. 6111666640660001116   61116664066001116   26._____
     7111300117001100733   7111300117001100733
     26666446664476518   26666446664476518

Questions 27-30.

DIRECTIONS: Questions 27 through 30 are to be answered by picking the answer which is in the correct numerical order, from the lowest number to the highest number, in each question.

27.   A.   44533, 44518, 44516, 44547   27._____
     B.   44516, 44518, 44533, 44547
     C.   44547, 44533, 44518, 44516
     D.   44518, 44516, 44547, 44533

28.   A.   95587, 95593, 95601, 95620   28._____
     B.   95601, 95620, 95587, 95593
     C.   95593, 95587, 95601, 95620
     D.   95620, 95601, 95593, 95587

29.   A.   232212, 232208, 232232, 232223   29._____
     B.   232208, 232223, 232212, 232232
     C.   232208, 232212, 232223, 232232
     D.   232223, 232232, 232208, 232212

30.   A.   113419, 113521, 113462, 113588   30._____
     B.   113588, 113462, 113521, 113419
     C.   113521, 113588, 113419, 113462
     D.   113419, 113462, 113521, 113588

KEY (CORRECT ANSWERS)

1.	C	11.	A	21.	C
2.	B	12.	C	22.	A
3.	D	13.	A	23.	D
4.	A	14.	A	24.	A
5.	C	15.	C	25.	C
6.	B	16.	B	26.	C
7.	D	17.	B	27.	B
8.	A	18.	B	28.	A
9.	D	19.	B	29.	C
10.	C	20.	B	30.	D

PREPARING WRITTEN MATERIALS

EXAMINATION SECTION
TEST 1

DIRECTIONS: Each of the following questions consists of a sentence which may be classified appropriately under one of the following four categories:
  A. Incorrect because of faulty grammar or sentence structure
  B. Incorrect because of faulty punctuation
  C. Incorrect because of faulty spelling or capitalization
  D. Correct

Examine each sentence carefully. Then, in the space at the right, print the letter preceding the best of the four alternatives suggested above. All incorrect sentences contain but one type of error. Consider a sentence correct if it contains none of the types of errors mentioned, even though there may be other correct ways of expressing the same thought.

1. The fire apparently started in the storeroom, which is usually locked.   1.____

2. On approaching the victim two bruises were noticed by this officer.   2.____

3. The officer, who was there examined the report with great care.   3.____

4. Each employee in the office had a separate desk.   4.____

5. Each employee in the office had a separate desk.   5.____

6. The suggested procedure is similar to the one now in use.   6.____

7. No one was more pleased with the new procedure than the chauffeur.   7.____

8. He tried to pursuade her to change the procedure.   8.____

9. The total of the expenses charged to petty cash were high.   9.____

10. An understanding between him and I was finally reached.   10.____

11. It was at the supervisor's request that the clerk agreed to postpone his vacation.   11.____

12. We do not believe that it is necessary for both he and the clerk to attend the conference.   12.____

13. All employees, who display perseverance, will be given adequate recognition.   13.____

14. He regrets that some of us employees are dissatisfied with our new assignments.   14.____

15. "Do you think that the raise was merited," asked the supervisor?   15.____

16. The new manual of procedure is a valuable supplament to our rules and regulation.   16.____

17. The typist admitted that she had attempted to pursuade the other employees to assist her in her work.   17.____

18. The supervisor asked that all amendments to the regulations be handled by you and I.   18.____

19. They told both he and I that the prisoner had escaped.   19.____

20. Any superior officer, who, disregards the just complaints of his subordinates, is remiss in the performance of his duty.   20.____

21. Only those members of the national organization who resided in the Middle west attended the conference in Chicago.   21.____

22. We told him to give the investigation assignment to whoever was available.   22.____

23. Please do not disappoint and embarass us by not appearing in court.   23.____

24. Despite the efforts of the Supervising mechanic, the elevator could not be started.   24.____

25. The U.S. Weather Bureau, weather record for the accident date was checked.   25.____

_____

KEY (CORRECT ANSWERS)

1.	D		11.	D
2.	A		12.	A
3.	B		13.	B
4.	D		14.	D
5.	B		15.	B
6.	C		16.	C
7.	D		17.	C
8.	C		18.	A
9.	A		19.	A
10.	A		20.	B

21.	C
22.	D
23.	C
24.	C
25.	B

_____

TEST 2

DIRECTIONS: Each question consists of a sentence. Some of the sentences contain errors in English grammar or usage, punctuation, spelling, or capitalization. A sentence does not contain an error simply because it could be written in a different manner. Choose answer

    A.   If the sentence contains an error in English grammar or usage
    B.   If the sentence contains an error in punctuation
    C.   If the sentence contains an error in spelling or capitalization
    D.   If the sentence does not contain any errors.

1. The severity of the sentence prescribed by contemporary statutes - including both the former and the revised New York Penal Laws - do not depend on what crime was intended by the offender. 1._____

2. It is generally recognized that two defects in the early law of attempt played a part in the birth of burglary: (1) immunity from prosecution for conduct short of the last act before completion of the crime, and (2) the relatively minor penalty imposed for an attempt (it being a common law misdemeanor) vis-a-vis the completed offense. 2._____

3. The first sentence of the statute is applicable to employees who enter their place of employment, invited guests, and all other persons who have an express or implied license or privilege to enter the premises. 3._____

4. Contemporary criminal codes in the United States generally divide burglary into various degrees, differentiating the categories according to place, time and other attendent circumstances. 4._____

5. The assignment was completed in record time but the payroll for it has not yet been preparid. 5._____

6. The operator, on the other hand, is willing to learn me how to use the mimeograph. 6._____

7. She is the prettiest of the three sisters. 7._____

8. She doesn't know; if the mail has arrived. 8._____

9. The doorknob of the office door is broke. 9._____

10. Although the department's supply of scratch pads and stationery have diminished considerably, the allotment for our division has not been reduced. 10._____

11. You have not told us whom you wish to designate as your secretary. 11._____

12. Upon reading the minutes of the last meeting, the new proposal was taken up for consideration. 12._____

13. Before beginning the discussion, we locked the door as a precautionery measure. 13._____

14. The supervisor remarked, "Only those clerks, who perform routine work, are permitted to take a rest period." 14._____

15. Not only will this duplicating machine make accurate copies, but it will also produce a quantity of work equal to fifteen transcribing typists. 15._____

16. "Mr. Jones," said the supervisor, "we regret our inability to grant you an extent ion of your leave of absence."   16._____

17. Although the employees find the work monotonous and fatigueing, they rarely complain.   17._____

18. We completed the tabulation of the receipts on time despite the fact that Miss Smith our fastest operator was absent for over a week.   18._____

19. The reaction of the employees who attended the meeting, as well as the reaction of those who did not attend, indicates clearly that the schedule is satisfactory to everyone concerned.   19._____

20. Of the two employees, the one in our office is the most efficient.   20._____

21. No one can apply or even understand, the new rules and regulations.   21._____

22. A large amount of supplies were stored in the empty office.   22._____

23. If an employee is occassionally asked to work overtime, he should do so willingly.   23._____

24. It is true that the new procedures are difficult to use but, we are certain that you will learn them quickly.   24._____

25. The office manager said that he did not know who would be given a large allotment under the new plan.   25._____

KEY (CORRECT ANSWERS)

1. A		11. D	
2. D		12. A	
3. D		13. C	
4. C		14. B	
5. C		15. A	
6. A		16. C	
7. D		17. C	
8. B		18. B	
9. A		19. D	
10. A		20. A	

21. B
22. A
23. C
24. B
25. D

TEST 3

DIRECTIONS: Each of the following sentences may be classified MOST appropriately under one of the following our categories:
- A. faulty because of incorrect grammar;
- B. faulty because of incorrect punctuation;
- C. faulty because of incorrect capitalization;
- D. correct

Examine each sentence carefully. Then, in the space at the right, print the capital letter preceding the option which is the BEST of the four suggested above. All incorrect sentences contain but one type of error. Consider a sentence correct if it contains none of the types of errors mentioned, even though there may be other correct ways of expressing the same thought.

1. The desk, as well as the chairs, were moved out of the office.   1._____

2. The clerk whose production was greatest for the month won a day's vacation as first prize.   2._____

3. Upon entering the room, the employees were found hard at work at their desks.   3._____

4. John Smith our new employee always arrives at work on time.   4._____

5. Punish whoever is guilty of stealing the money.   5._____

6. Intelligent and persistent effort lead to success no matter what the job may be.   6._____

7. The secretary asked, "can you call again at three o'clock?"   7._____

8. He told us, that if the report was not accepted at the next meeting, it would have to be rewritten.   8._____

9. He would not have sent the letter if he had known that it would cause so much excitement.   9._____

10. We all looked forward to him coming to visit us.   10._____

11. If you find that you are unable to complete the assignment please notify me as soon as possible.   11._____

12. Every girl in the office went home on time but me; there was still some work for me to finish.   12._____

13. He wanted to know who the letter was addressed to, Mr. Brown or Mr. Smith.   13._____

14. "Mr. Jones, he said, please answer this letter as soon as possible."   14._____

15. The new clerk had an unusual accent inasmuch as he was born and educated in the south.   15._____

16. Although he is younger than her, he earns a higher salary.   16._____

17. Neither of the two administrators are going to attend the conference being held in Washington, D.C.   17.____

18. Since Miss Smith and Miss Jones have more experience than us, they have been given more responsible duties.   18.____

19. Mr. Shaw the supervisor of the stock room maintains an inventory of stationery and office supplies.   19.____

20. Inasmuch as this matter affects both you and I, we should take joint action.   20.____

21. Who do you think will be able to perform this highly technical work?   21.____

22. Of the two employees, John is considered the most competent.   22.____

23. He is not coming home on tuesday; we expect him next week.   23.____

24. Stenographers, as well as typists must be able to type rapidly and accurately.   24.____

25. Having been placed in the safe we were sure that the money would not be stolen.   25.____

_____

KEY (CORRECT ANSWERS)

1.	A	11.	B
2.	D	12.	D
3.	A	13.	A
4.	B	14.	B
5.	D	15.	C
6.	A	16.	A
7.	C	17.	A
8.	A	18.	A
9.	D	19.	B
10.	A	20.	A

21.	D
22.	A
23.	C
24.	B
25.	A

_____

TEST 4

DIRECTIONS: Each of the following sentences consist of four sentences lettered A, B, C, and D. One of the sentences in each group contains an error in grammar or punctuation. Indicate the INCORRECT sentence in each group. *PRINT THE LETTER OF THE CORRECT ANSWER IN THE SPACE AT THE RIGHT.*

1. A. Give the message to whoever is on duty.
   B. The teacher who's pupil won first prize presented the award.
   C. Between you and me, I don't expect the program to succeed.
   D. His running to catch the bus caused the accident.

   1.____

2. A. The process, which was patented only last year is already obsolete.
   B. His interest in science (which continues to the present) led him to convert his basement into a laboratory.
   C. He described the book as "verbose, repetitious, and bombastic".
   D. Our new director will need to possess three qualities: vision, patience, and fortitude.

   2.____

3. A. The length of ladder trucks varies considerably.
   B. The probationary fireman reported to the officer to whom he was assigned.
   C. The lecturer emphasized the need for we firemen to be punctual.
   D. Neither the officers nor the members of the company knew about the new procedure.

   3.____

4. A. Ham and eggs is the specialty of the house.
   B. He is one of the students who are on probation.
   C. Do you think that either one of us have a chance to be nominated for president of the class?
   D. I assume that either he was to be in charge or you were.

   4.____

5. A. Its a long road that has no turn.
   B. To run is more tiring than to walk.
   C. We have been assigned three new reports: namely, the statistical summary, the narrative summary, and the budgetary summary.
   D. Had the first payment been made in January, the second would be due in April.

   5.____

6. A. Each employer has his own responsibilities.
   B. If a person speaks correctly, they make a good impression.
   C. Every one of the operators has had her vacation.
   D. Has anybody filed his report?

   6.____

7. A. The manager, with all his salesmen, was obliged to go.
   B. Who besides them is to sign the agreement?
   C. One report without the others is incomplete.
   D. Several clerks, as well as the proprietor, was injured.

   7.____

8. A. A suspension of these activities is expected.
   B. The machine is economical because first cost and upkeep are low.
   C. A knowledge of stenography and filing are required for this position.
   D. The condition in which the goods were received shows that the packing was not done properly.

   8.____

9. A. There seems to be a great many reasons for disagreement.   9.____
    B. It does not seem possible that they could have failed.
    C. Have there always been too few applicants for these positions?
    D. There is no excuse for these errors.

10. A. We shall be pleased to answer your question.   10.____
    B. Shall we plan the meeting for Saturday?
    C. I will call you promptly at seven.
    D. Can I borrow your book after you have read it?

11. A. You are as capable as I.   11.____
    B. Everyone is willing to sign but him and me.
    C. As for he and his assistant, I cannot praise them too highly.
    D. Between you and me, I think he will be dismissed.

12. A. Our competitors bid above us last week.   12.____
    B. The survey which was began last year has not yet been completed.
    C. The operators had shown that they understood their instructions.
    D. We have never ridden over worse roads.

13. A. Who did they say was responsible?   13.____
    B. Whom did you suspect?
    C. Who do you suppose it was?
    D. Whom do you mean?

14. A. Of the two propositions, this is the worse.   14.____
    B. Which report do you consider the best -- the one in January or the one in July?
    C. I believe this is the most practicable of the many plans submitted.
    D. He is the youngest employee in the organization.

15. A. The firm had but three orders last week.   15.____
    B. That doesn't really seem possible.
    C. After twenty years scarcely none of the old business remains.
    D. Has he done nothing about it?

KEY (CORRECT ANSWERS)

1.	B		6.	B
2.	A		7.	D
3.	C		8.	C
4.	C		9.	A
5.	A		10.	D

11.	C
12.	B
13.	A
14.	B
15.	C

PREPARING WRITTEN MATERIAL

PARAGRAPH REARRANGEMENT
COMMENTARY

The sentences which follow are in scrambled order. You are to rearrange them in proper order and indicate the letter choice containing the correct answer at the space at the right.

Each group of sentences in this section is actually a paragraph presented in scrambled order. Each sentence in the group has a place in that paragraph; no sentence is to be left out. You are to read each group of sentences and decide upon the best order in which to put the sentences so as to form as well-organized paragraph.

The questions in this section measure the ability to solve a problem when all the facts relevant to its solution are not given.

More specifically, certain positions of responsibility and authority require the employee to discover connections between events sometimes, apparently, unrelated. In order to do this, the employee will find it necessary to correctly infer that unspecified events have probably occurred or are likely to occur. This ability becomes especially important when action must be taken on incomplete information.

Accordingly, these questions require competitors to choose among several suggested alternatives, each of which presents a different sequential arrangement of the events. Competitors must choose the MOST logical of the suggested sequences.

In order to do so, they may be required to draw on general knowledge to infer missing concepts or events that are essential to sequencing the given events. Competitors should be careful to infer only what is essential to the sequence. The plausibility of the wrong alternatives will always require the inclusion of unlikely events or of additional chains of events which are NOT essential to sequencing the given events.

It's very important to remember that you are looking for the best of the four possible choices, and that the best choice of all may not even be one of the answers you're given to choose from.

There is no one right way to solve these problems. Many people have found it helpful to first write out the order of the sentences, as they would have arranged them, on their scrap paper before looking at the possible answers. If their optimum answer is there, this can save them some time. If it isn't, this method can still give insight into solving the problem. Others find it most helpful to just go through each of the possible choices, contrasting each as they go along. You should use whatever method feels comfortable, and works, for you.

While most of these types of questions are not that difficult, we've added a higher percentage of the difficult type, just to give you more practice. Usually there are only one or two questions on this section that contain such subtle distinctions that you're unable to answer confidently, and you then may find yourself stuck deciding between two possible choices, neither of which you're sure about.

EXAMINATION SECTION
TEST 1

DIRECTIONS: Each question consists of several sentences which can be arranged in a logi-cal sequence. For each question, select the choice which places the num-bered sentences in the MOST logical sequence. *PRINT THE LETTER OF THE CORRECT ANSWER IN THE SPACE AT THE RIGHT.*

1. I.   A body was found in the woods.
    II. A man proclaimed innocence.
    III. The owner of a gun was located.
    IV. A gun was traced.
    V.   The owner of a gun was questioned.
    The CORRECT answer is:

    A. IV, III, V, II, I   B. II, I, IV, III, V
    C. I, IV, III, V, II   D. I, III, V, II, IV
    E. I, II, IV, III, V

1.____

2. I.   A man was in a hunting accident.
    II. A man fell down a flight of steps.
    III. A man lost his vision in one eye.
    IV. A man broke his leg.
    V.   A man had to walk with a cane.
    The CORRECT answer is:

    A. II, IV, V, I, III   B. IV, V, I, III, II
    C. III, I, IV, V, II   D. I, III, V, II, IV
    E. I, III, II, IV, V

2.____

3. I.   A man is offered a new job.
    II. A woman is offered a new job.
    III. A man works as a waiter.
    IV. A woman works as a waitress.
    V.   A woman gives notice.
    The CORRECT answer is:

    A. IV, II, V, III, I   B. IV, II, V, I, III
    C. II, IV, V, III, I   D. III, I, IV, II, V
    E. IV, III, II, V, I

3.____

4. I.   A train left the station late.
    II. A man was late for work.
    III. A man lost his job.
    IV. Many people complained because the train was late.
    V.   There was a traffic jam.
    The CORRECT answer is:

    A. V, II, I, IV, III   B. V, I, IV, II, III
    C. V, I, II, IV, III   D. I, V, IV, II, III
    E. II, I, IV, V, III

4.____

5. I.   The burden of proof as to each issue is determined before trial and remains upon   5.____
          the same party throughout the trial.
    II.   The jury is at liberty to believe one witness' testimony as against a number of
          contradictory witnesses.
    III.   In a civil case, the party bearing the burden of proof is required to prove his con-
          tention by a fair preponderance of the evidence.
    IV.   However, it must be noted that a fair preponderance of evidence does not neces-
          sarily mean a greater number of witnesses.
    V.   The burden of proof is the burden which rests upon one of the parties to an
          action to persuade the trier of the facts, generally the jury, that a proposition he
          asserts is true.
    VI.   If the evidence is equally balanced, or if it leaves the jury in such doubt as to be
          unable to decide the controversy either way, judgment must be given against the
          party upon whom the burden of proof rests.
    The CORRECT answer is:

    A. III, II, V, IV, I, VI   B. I, II,VI,V,III,IV
    C. III, IV, V, I, II, VI   D. V, I, III,VI, IV, II
    E. I,V, III, VI, IV, II

6. I.   If a parent is without assets and is unemployed, he cannot be convicted of the   6.____
          crime of non-support of a child.
    II.   The term *sufficient ability* has been held to mean sufficient financial ability.
    III.   It does not matter if his unemployment is by choice or unavoidable circum-
          stances.
    IV.   If he fails to take any steps at all, he may be liable to prosecution for endangering
          the welfare of a child.
    V.   Under the penal law, a parent is responsible for the support of his minor child
          only if the parent is of *sufficient ability*.
    VI.   An indigent parent may meet his obligation by borrowing money or by seeking
          aid under the provisions of the Social Welfare Law.
    The CORRECT answer is:

    A. VI, I, V, III, II, IV   B. I, III, V, II, IV, VI
    C. V, II, I, III, VI, IV   D. I, VI, IV, V, II, III
    E. II, V, I, III, VI, IV

7. I.   Consider, for example, the case of a rabble rouser who urges a group of twenty   7.____
          people to go out and break the windows of a nearby factory.
    II.   Therefore, the law fills the indicated gap with the crime of *inciting to riot*.
    III.   A person is considered guilty of inciting to riot when he urges ten or more per-
          sons to engage in tumultuous and violent conduct of a kind likely to create public
          alarm.
    IV.   However, if he has not obtained the cooperation of at least four people, he can-
          not be charged with unlawful assembly.
    V.   The charge of inciting to riot was added to the law to cover types of conduct
          which cannot be classified as either the crime of *riot* or the crime of *unlawful
          assembly*.
    VI.   If he acquires the acquiescence of at least four of them, he is guilty of unlawful
          assembly even if the project does not materialize.
    The CORRECT answer is:

A. III, V, I, VI, IV, II
B. V, I, IV, VI, II, III
C. III, IV, I, V, II, VI
D. V, I, IV, VI, III, II
E. V, III, I, VI, IV, II

8. I. If, however, the rebuttal evidence presents an issue of credibility, it is for the jury to determine whether the presumption has, in fact, been destroyed.
    II. Once sufficient evidence to the contrary is introduced, the presumption disappears from the trial.
    III. The effect of a presumption is to place the burden upon the adversary to come forward with evidence to rebut the presumption.
    IV. When a presumption is overcome and ceases to exist in the case, the fact or facts which gave rise to the presumption still remain.
    V. Whether a presumption has been overcome is ordinarily a question for the court.
    VI. Such information may furnish a basis for a logical inference.

The CORRECT answer is:

A. IV, VI, II, V, I, III
B. III, II, V, I, IV, VI
C. V, III, VI, IV, II, I
D. V, IV, I, II, VI, III
E. II, III, V, I, IV, VI

8.____

9. I. An executive may answer a letter by writing his reply on the face of the letter itself instead of having a return letter typed.
    II. This procedure is efficient because it saves the executive's time, the typist's time, and saves office file space.
    III. Copying machines are used in small offices as well as large offices to save time and money in making brief replies to business letters.
    IV. A copy is made on a copying machine to go into the company files, while the original is mailed back to the sender.

The CORRECT answer is:

A. I, II, IV, III
B. I, IV, II, III
C. III, I, IV, II
D. III, IV, II, I

9.____

10. I. Most organizations favor one of the types but always include the others to a lesser degree.
    II. However, we can detect a definite trend toward greater use of symbolic control.
    III. We suggest that our local police agencies are today primarily utilizing material control.
    IV. Control can be classified into three types: physical, material, and symbolic.

The CORRECT answer is:

A. IV, II, III, I
B. II, I, IV, III
C. III, IV, II, I
D. IV, I, III, II

10.____

11. I. Project residents had first claim to this use, followed by surrounding neighborhood children.
    II. By contrast, recreation space within the project's interior was found to be used more often by both groups.
    III. Studies of the use of project grounds in many cities showed grounds left open for public use were neglected and unused, both by residents and by members of the surrounding community.

11.____

IV. Project residents had clearly laid claim to the play spaces, setting up and enforcing unwritten rules for use.

V. Each group, by experience, found their activities easily disrupted by other groups, and their claim to the use of space for recreation difficult to enforce.

The CORRECT answer is:

A. IV, V, I, II, III
C. I, IV, III, II, V
B. V, II, IV, III, I
D. III, V, II, IV, I

12.
I. They do not consider the problems correctable within the existing subsidy formula and social policy of accepting all eligible applicants regardless of social behavior and lifestyle.

II. A recent survey, however, indicated that tenants believe these problems correctable by local housing authorities and management within the existing financial formula.

III. Many of the problems and complaints concerning public housing management and design have created resentment between the tenant and the landlord.

IV. This same survey indicated that administrators and managers do not agree with the tenants.

The CORRECT answer is:

A. II, I, III, IV
C. III, II, IV, I
B. I, III, IV, II
D. IV, II, I, III

12._____

13.
I. In single-family residences, there is usually enough distance between tenants to prevent occupants from annoying one another.

II. For example, a certain small percentage of tenant families has one or more members addicted to alcohol.

III. While managers believe in the right of individuals to live as they choose, the manager becomes concerned when the pattern of living jeopardizes others' rights.

IV. Still others turn night into day, staging lusty entertainments which carry on into the hours when most tenants are trying to sleep.

V. In apartment buildings, however, tenants live so closely together that any misbehavior can result in unpleasant living conditions.

VI. Other families engage in violent argument.

The CORRECT answer is:

A. III, II, V, IV, VI, I
C. II, V, IV, I, III, VI
B. I, V, II, VI, IV, III
D. IV, II, V, VI, III, I

13._____

14.
I. Congress made the commitment explicit in the Housing Act of 1949, establishing as a national goal the realization of *a decent home and suitable environment for every American family.*

II. The result has been that the goal of decent home and suitable environment is still as far distant as ever for the disadvantaged urban family.

III. In spite of this action by Congress, federal housing programs have continued to be fragmented and grossly underfunded.

IV. The passage of the National Housing Act signalled a new federal commitment to provide housing for the nation's citizens.

The CORRECT answer is:

A. I, IV, III, II
C. IV, I, II, III
B. IV, I, III, II
D. II, IV, I, III

14._____

15.   I.   The greater expense does not necessarily involve *exploitation,* but it is often per-   15.____
            ceived as exploitative and unfair by those who are aware of the price differences
            involved, but unaware of operating costs.
       II. Ghetto residents believe they are *exploited* by local merchants, and evidence
            substantiates some of these beliefs.
       III. However, stores in low-income areas were more likely to be small independents,
            which could not achieve the economies available to supermarket chains and
            were, therefore, more likely to charge higher prices, and the customers were
            more likely to buy smaller-sized packages which are more expensive per unit of
            measure.
       IV. A study conducted in one city showed that distinctly higher prices were charged
            for goods sold in ghetto stores than in other areas.
       The CORRECT answer is:

       A. IV, II, I, III   B. IV, I, III, II
       C. II, IV, III, I   D. II, III, IV, I

KEY (CORRECT ANSWERS)

1.	C		6.	C
2.	E		7.	A
3.	B		8.	B
4.	B		9.	C
5.	D		10.	D

11.	D
12.	C
13.	B
14.	B
15.	C

GLOSSARY OF LEGAL TERMS

TABLE OF CONTENTS

GLOSSARY OF LEGAL TERMS

A

ACTION - "Action" includes a civil action and a criminal action.

A FORTIORI - A term meaning you can reason one thing from the existence of certain facts.

A POSTERIORI - From what goes after; from effect to cause.

A PRIORI - From what goes before; from cause to effect.

AB INITIO - From the beginning.

ABATE - To diminish or put an end to.

ABET - To encourage the commission of a crime.

ABEYANCE - Suspension, temporary suppression.

ABIDE - To accept the consequences of.

ABJURE - To renounce; give up.

ABRIDGE - To reduce; contract; diminish.

ABROGATE - To annul, repeal, or destroy.

ABSCOND - To hide or absent oneself to avoid legal action.

ABSTRACT - A summary.

ABUT - To border on, to touch.

ACCESS - Approach; in real property law it means the right of the owner of property to the use of the highway or road next to his land, without obstruction by intervening property owners.

ACCESSORY - In criminal law, it means the person who contributes or aids in the commission of a crime.

ACCOMMODATED PARTY - One to whom credit is extended on the strength of another person signing a commercial paper.

ACCOMMODATION PAPER - A commercial paper to which the accommodating party has put his name.

ACCOMPLICE - In criminal law, it means a person who together with the principal offender commits a crime.

ACCORD - An agreement to accept something different or less than that to which one is entitled, which extinguishes the entire obligation.

ACCOUNT - A statement of mutual demands in the nature of debt and credit between parties.

ACCRETION - The act of adding to a thing; in real property law, it means gradual accumulation of land by natural causes.

ACCRUE - To grow to; to be added to.

ACKNOWLEDGMENT - The act of going before an official authorized to take acknowledgments, and acknowledging an act as one's own.

ACQUIESCENCE - A silent appearance of consent.

ACQUIT - To legally determine the innocence of one charged with a crime.

AD INFINITUM - Indefinitely.

AD LITEM - For the suit.

AD VALOREM - According to value.

ADJECTIVE LAW - Rules of procedure.

ADJUDICATION - The judgment given in a case.

ADMIRALTY - Court having jurisdiction over maritime cases.

ADULT - Sixteen years old or over (in criminal law).

ADVANCE - In commercial law, it means to pay money or render other value before it is due.

ADVERSE - Opposed; contrary.

ADVOCATE -   (v.) To speak in favor of;
              (n.) One who assists, defends, or pleads for another.

AFFIANT - A person who makes and signs an affidavit.

AFFIDAVIT - A written and sworn to declaration of facts, voluntarily made.

AFFINITY- The relationship between persons through marriage with the kindred of each other; distinguished from consanguinity, which is the relationship by blood.

AFFIRM - To ratify; also when an appellate court affirms a judgment, decree, or order, it means that it is valid and right and must stand as rendered in the lower court.

AFOREMENTIONED; AFORESAID - Before or already said.

AGENT - One who represents and acts for another.

AID AND COMFORT - To help; encourage.

ALIAS - A name not one's true name.

ALIBI - A claim of not being present at a certain place at a certain time.

ALLEGE - To assert.

ALLOTMENT - A share or portion.

AMBIGUITY - Uncertainty; capable of being understood in more than one way.

AMENDMENT - Any language made or proposed as a change in some principal writing.

AMICUS CURIAE - A friend of the court; one who has an interest in a case, although not a party in the case, who volunteers advice upon matters of law to the judge. For example, a brief amicus curiae.

AMORTIZATION - To provide for a gradual extinction of (a future obligation) in advance of maturity, especially, by periodical contributions to a sinking fund which will be adequate to discharge a debt or make a replacement when it becomes necessary.

ANCILLARY - Aiding, auxiliary.

ANNOTATION - A note added by way of comment or explanation.

ANSWER - A written statement made by a defendant setting forth the grounds of his defense.

ANTE - Before.

ANTE MORTEM - Before death.

APPEAL - The removal of a case from a lower court to one of superior jurisdiction for the purpose of obtaining a review.

APPEARANCE - Coming into court as a party to a suit.

APPELLANT - The party who takes an appeal from one court or jurisdiction to another (appellate) court for review.

APPELLEE - The party against whom an appeal is taken.

APPROPRIATE - To make a thing one's own.

APPROPRIATION - Prescribing the destination of a thing; the act of the legislature designating a particular fund, to be applied to some object of government expenditure.

APPURTENANT - Belonging to; accessory or incident to.

ARBITER - One who decides a dispute; a referee.

ARBITRARY - Unreasoned; not governed by any fixed rules or standard.

ARGUENDO - By way of argument.

ARRAIGN - To call the prisoner before the court to answer to a charge.

ASSENT - A declaration of willingness to do something in compliance with a request.

ASSERT - Declare.

ASSESS - To fix the rate or amount.

ASSIGN - To transfer; to appoint; to select for a particular purpose.

ASSIGNEE - One who receives an assignment.

ASSIGNOR - One who makes an assignment.

AT BAR - Before the court.

AT ISSUE - When parties in an action come to a point where one asserts something and the other denies it.

ATTACH - Seize property by court order and sometimes arrest a person.

ATTEST - To witness a will, etc.; act of attestation.

AVERMENT - A positive statement of facts.

B

BAIL - To obtain the release of a person from legal custody by giving security and promising that he shall appear in court; to deliver (goods, etc.) in trust to a person for a special purpose.

BAILEE - One to whom personal property is delivered under a contract of bailment.

BAILMENT - Delivery of personal property to another to be held for a certain purpose and to be returned when the purpose is accomplished.

BAILOR - The party who delivers goods to another, under a contract of bailment.

BANC (OR BANK) - Bench; the place where a court sits permanently or regularly; also the assembly of all the judges of a court.

BANKRUPT - An insolvent person, technically, one declared to be bankrupt after a bankruptcy proceeding.

BAR - The legal profession.

BARRATRY - Exciting groundless judicial proceedings.

BARTER - A contract by which parties exchange goods for other goods.

BATTERY - Illegal interfering with another's person.

BEARER - In commercial law, it means the person in possession of a commercial paper which is payable to the bearer.

BENCH - The court itself or the judge.

BENEFICIARY - A person benefiting under a will, trust, or agreement.

BEST EVIDENCE RULE, THE - Except as otherwise provided by statute, no evidence other than the writing itself is admissible to prove the content of a writing. This section shall be known and may be cited as the best evidence rule.

BEQUEST - A gift of personal property under a will.

BILL - A formal written statement of complaint to a court of justice; also, a draft of an act of the legislature before it becomes a law; also, accounts for goods sold, services rendered, or work done.

BONA FIDE - In or with good faith; honestly.

BOND - An instrument by which the maker promises to pay a sum of money to another, usually providing that upon performances of a certain condition the obligation shall be void.

BOYCOTT - A plan to prevent the carrying on of a business by wrongful means.

BREACH - The breaking or violating of a law, or the failure to carry out a duty.

BRIEF - A written document, prepared by a lawyer to serve as the basis of an argument upon a case in court, usually an appellate court.

BURDEN OF PRODUCING EVIDENCE - The obligation of a party to introduce evidence sufficient to avoid a ruling against him on the issue.

BURDEN OF PROOF - The obligation of a party to establish by evidence a requisite degree of belief concerning a fact in the mind of the trier of fact or the court. The burden of proof may require a party to raise a reasonable doubt concerning the existence of nonexistence of a fact or that he establish the existence or nonexistence of a fact by a preponderance of the evidence, by clear and convincing proof, or by proof beyond a reasonable doubt.

Except as otherwise provided by law, the burden of proof requires proof by a preponderance of the evidence.

BUSINESS, A - Shall include every kind of business, profession, occupation, calling or operation of institutions, whether carried on for profit or not.

BY-LAWS - Regulations, ordinances, or rules enacted by a corporation, association, etc., for its own government.

C

CANON - A doctrine; also, a law or rule, of a church or association in particular.

CAPIAS - An order to arrest.

CAPTION - In a pleading, deposition or other paper connected with a case in court, it is the heading or introductory clause which shows the names of the parties, name of the court, number of the case on the docket or calendar, etc.

CARRIER - A person or corporation undertaking to transport persons or property.

CASE - A general term for an action, cause, suit, or controversy before a judicial body.

CAUSE - A suit, litigation or action before a court.

CAVEAT EMPTOR - Let the buyer beware. This term expresses the rule that the purchaser of an article must examine, judge, and test it for himself, being bound to discover any obvious defects or imperfections.

CERTIFICATE - A written representation that some legal formality has been complied with.

CERTIORARI - To be informed of; the name of a writ issued by a superior court directing the lower court to send up to the former the record and proceedings of a case.

CHANGE OF VENUE - To remove place of trial from one place to another.

CHARGE - An obligation or duty; a formal complaint; an instruction of the court to the jury upon a case.

CHARTER - (n.) The authority by virtue of which an organized body acts; (v.) in mercantile law, it means to hire or lease a vehicle or vessel for transportation.

CHATTEL - An article of personal property.

CHATTEL MORTGAGE - A mortgage on personal property.

CIRCUIT - A division of the country, for the administration of justice; a geographical area served by a court.

CITATION - The act of the court by which a person is summoned or cited; also, a reference to legal authority.

CIVIL (ACTIONS)- It indicates the private rights and remedies of individuals in contrast to the word "criminal" (actions) which relates to prosecution for violation of laws.

CLAIM (n.) - Any demand held or asserted as of right.

CODICIL - An addition to a will.

CODIFY - To arrange the laws of a country into a code.

COGNIZANCE - Notice or knowledge.

COLLATERAL - By the side; accompanying; an article or thing given to secure performance of a promise.

COMITY - Courtesy; the practice by which one court follows the decision of another court on the same question.

COMMIT - To perform, as an act; to perpetrate, as a crime; to send a person to prison.

COMMON LAW - As distinguished from law created by the enactment of the legislature (called statutory law), it relates to those principles and rules of action which derive their authority solely from usages and customs of immemorial antiquity, particularly with reference to the ancient unwritten law of England. The written pronouncements of the common law are found in court decisions.

COMMUTE - Change punishment to one less severe.

COMPLAINANT - One who applies to the court for legal redress.

COMPLAINT - The pleading of a plaintiff in a civil action; or a charge that a person has committed a specified offense.

COMPROMISE - An arrangement for settling a dispute by agreement.

CONCUR - To agree, consent.

CONCURRENT - Running together, at the same time.

CONDEMNATION - Taking private property for public use on payment therefor.

CONDITION - Mode or state of being; a qualification or restriction.

CONDUCT - Active and passive behavior; both verbal and nonverbal.

CONFESSION - Voluntary statement of guilt of crime.

CONFIDENTIAL COMMUNICATION BETWEEN CLIENT AND LAWYER - Information transmitted between a client and his lawyer in the course of that relationship and in confidence by a means which, so far as the client is aware, discloses the information to no third persons other than those who are present to further the interest of the client in the consultation or those to whom disclosure is reasonably necessary for the transmission of the information or the accomplishment of the purpose for which the lawyer is consulted, and includes a legal opinion formed and the advice given by the lawyer in the course of that relationship.

CONFRONTATION - Witness testifying in presence of defendant.

CONSANGUINITY - Blood relationship.

CONSIGN - To give in charge; commit; entrust; to send or transmit goods to a merchant, factor, or agent for sale.

CONSIGNEE - One to whom a consignment is made.

CONSIGNOR - One who sends or makes a consignment.

CONSPIRACY - In criminal law, it means an agreement between two or more persons to commit an unlawful act.

CONSPIRATORS - Persons involved in a conspiracy.

CONSTITUTION - The fundamental law of a nation or state.

CONSTRUCTION OF GENDERS - The masculine gender includes the feminine and neuter.

CONSTRUCTION OF SINGULAR AND PLURAL - The singular number includes the plural; and the plural, the singular.

CONSTRUCTION OF TENSES - The present tense includes the past and future tenses; and the future, the present.

CONSTRUCTIVE - An act or condition assumed from other parts or conditions.

CONSTRUE - To ascertain the meaning of language.

CONSUMMATE - To complete.

CONTIGUOUS - Adjoining; touching; bounded by.

CONTINGENT - Possible, but not assured; dependent upon some condition.

CONTINUANCE - The adjournment or postponement of an action pending in a court.

CONTRA - Against, opposed to; contrary.

CONTRACT - An agreement between two or more persons to do or not to do a particular thing.

CONTROVERT - To dispute, deny.

CONVERSION - Dealing with the personal property of another as if it were one's own, without right.

CONVEYANCE - An instrument transferring title to land.

CONVICTION - Generally, the result of a criminal trial which ends in a judgment or sentence that the defendant is guilty as charged.

COOPERATIVE - A cooperative is a voluntary organization of persons with a common interest, formed and operated along democratic lines for the purpose of supplying services at cost to its members and other patrons, who contribute both capital and business.

CORPUS DELICTI - The body of a crime; the crime itself.

CORROBORATE - To strengthen; to add weight by additional evidence.

COUNTERCLAIM - A claim presented by a defendant in opposition to or deduction from the claim of the plaintiff.

COUNTY - Political subdivision of a state.

COVENANT - Agreement.

CREDIBLE - Worthy of belief.

CREDITOR - A person to whom a debt is owing by another person, called the "debtor."

CRIMINAL ACTION - Includes criminal proceedings.

CRIMINAL INFORMATION - Same as complaint.

CRITERION (sing.)

CRITERIA (plural) - A means or tests for judging; a standard or standards.

CROSS-EXAMINATION - Examination of a witness by a party other than the direct examiner upon a matter that is within the scope of the direct examination of the witness.

CULPABLE - Blamable.

CY-PRES - As near as (possible). The rule of *cy-pres* is a rule for the construction of instruments in equity by which the intention of the party is carried out *as near as may be*, when it would be impossible or illegal to give it literal effect.

D

DAMAGES - A monetary compensation, which may be recovered in the courts by any person who has suffered loss, or injury, whether to his person, property or rights through the unlawful act or omission or negligence of another.

DECLARANT - A person who makes a statement.

DE FACTO - In fact; actually but without legal authority.

DE JURE - Of right; legitimate; lawful.

DE MINIMIS - Very small or trifling.

DE NOVO - Anew; afresh; a second time.

DEBT - A specified sum of money owing to one person from another, including not only the obligation of the debtor to pay, but the right of the creditor to receive and enforce payment.

DECEDENT - A dead person.

DECISION - A judgment or decree pronounced by a court in determination of a case.

DECREE - An order of the court, determining the rights of all parties to a suit.

DEED - A writing containing a contract sealed and delivered; particularly to convey real property.

DEFALCATION - Misappropriation of funds.

DEFAMATION - Injuring one's reputation by false statements.

DEFAULT - The failure to fulfill a duty, observe a promise, discharge an obligation, or perform an agreement.

DEFENDANT - The person defending or denying; the party against whom relief or recovery is sought in an action or suit.

DEFRAUD - To practice fraud; to cheat or trick.

DELEGATE (v.)- To entrust to the care or management of another.

DELICTUS - A crime.

DEMUR (v.) - To dispute the sufficiency in law of the pleading of the other side.

DEMURRAGE - In maritime law, it means, the sum fixed or allowed as remuneration to the owners of a ship for the detention of their vessel beyond the number of days allowed for loading and unloading or for sailing; also used in railroad terminology.

DENIAL - A form of pleading; refusing to admit the truth of a statement, charge, etc.

DEPONENT - One who gives testimony under oath reduced to writing.

DEPOSITION - Testimony given under oath outside of court for use in court or for the purpose of obtaining information in preparation for trial of a case.

DETERIORATION - A degeneration such as from decay, corrosion or disintegration.

DETRIMENT - Any loss or harm to person or property.

DEVIATION - A turning aside.

DEVISE - A gift of real property by the last will and testament of the donor.

DICTUM (sing.)

DICTA (plural) - Any statements made by the court in an opinion concerning some rule of law not necessarily involved nor essential to the determination of the case.

DIRECT EVIDENCE - Evidence that directly proves a fact, without an inference or presumption, and which in itself if true, conclusively establishes that fact.

DIRECT EXAMINATION - The first examination of a witness upon a matter that is not within the scope of a previous examination of the witness.

DISAFFIRM - To repudiate.

DISMISS - In an action or suit, it means to dispose of the case without any further consideration or hearing.

DISSENT - To denote disagreement of one or more judges of a court with the decision passed by the majority upon a case before them.

DOCKET (n.) - A formal record, entered in brief, of the proceedings in a court.

DOCTRINE - A rule, principle, theory of law.

DOMICILE - That place where a man has his true, fixed and permanent home to which whenever he is absent he has the intention of returning.

DRAFT (n.) - A commercial paper ordering payment of money drawn by one person on another.

DRAWEE - The person who is requested to pay the money.

DRAWER - The person who draws the commercial paper and addresses it to the drawee.

DUPLICATE - A counterpart produced by the same impression as the original enlargements and miniatures, or by mechanical or electronic re-recording, or by chemical reproduction, or by other equivalent technique which accurately reproduces the original.

DURESS - Use of force to compel performance or non-performance of an act.

E

EASEMENT - A liberty, privilege, or advantage without profit, in the lands of another.

EGRESS - Act or right of going out or leaving; emergence.

EIUSDEM GENERIS - Of the same kind, class or nature. A rule used in the construction of language in a legal document.

EMBEZZLEMENT - To steal; to appropriate fraudulently to one's own use property entrusted to one's care.

EMBRACERY - Unlawful attempt to influence jurors, etc., but not by offering value.

EMINENT DOMAIN - The right of a state to take private property for public use.

ENACT - To make into a law.

ENDORSEMENT - Act of writing one's name on the back of a note, bill or similar written instrument.

ENJOIN - To require a person, by writ of injunction from a court of equity, to perform or to abstain or desist from some act.

ENTIRETY - The whole; that which the law considers as one whole, and not capable of being divided into parts.

ENTRAPMENT - Inducing one to commit a crime so as to arrest him.

ENUMERATED - Mentioned specifically; designated.

ENURE - To operate or take effect.

EQUITY - In its broadest sense, this term denotes the spirit and the habit of fairness, justness, and right dealing which regulate the conduct of men.

ERROR - A mistake of law, or the false or irregular application of law as will nullify the judicial proceedings.

ESCROW - A deed, bond or other written engagement, delivered to a third person, to be delivered by him only upon the performance or fulfillment of some condition.

ESTATE - The interest which any one has in lands, or in any other subject of property.

ESTOP - To stop, bar, or impede.

ESTOPPEL - A rule of law which prevents a man from alleging or denying a fact, because of his own previous act.

ET AL. (alii) - And others.

ET SEQ. (sequential) - And the following.

ET UX. (uxor) - And wife.

EVIDENCE - Testimony, writings, material objects, or other things presented to the senses that are offered to prove the existence or non-existence of a fact.

Means from which inferences may be drawn as a basis of proof in duly constituted judicial or fact finding tribunals, and includes testimony in the form of opinion and hearsay.

EX CONTRACTU

EX DELICTO - In law, rights and causes of action are divided into two classes, those arising *ex contractu* (from a contract) and those arising *ex delicto* (from a delict or tort).

EX OFFICIO - From office; by virtue of the office.

EX PARTE - On one side only; by or for one.

EX POST FACTO - After the fact.

EX POST FACTO LAW - A law passed after an act was done which retroactively makes such act a crime.

EX REL. (relations) - Upon relation or information.

EXCEPTION - An objection upon a matter of law to a decision made, either before or after judgment by a court.

EXECUTOR (male)

EXECUTRIX (female) - A person who has been appointed by will to execute the will.

EXECUTORY - That which is yet to be executed or performed.

EXEMPT - To release from some liability to which others are subject.

EXONERATION - The removal of a burden, charge or duty.

EXTRADITION - Surrender of a fugitive from one nation to another.

F

F.A.S.- "Free alongside ship"; delivery at dock for ship named.

F.O.B.- "Free on board"; seller will deliver to car, truck, vessel, or other conveyance by which goods are to be transported, without expense or risk of loss to the buyer or consignee.

FABRICATE - To construct; to invent a false story.

FACSIMILE - An exact or accurate copy of an original instrument.

FACTOR - A commercial agent.

FEASANCE - The doing of an act.

FELONIOUS - Criminal, malicious.

FELONY - Generally, a criminal offense that may be punished by death or imprisonment for more than one year as differentiated from a misdemeanor.

FEME SOLE - A single woman.

FIDUCIARY - A person who is invested with rights and powers to be exercised for the benefit of another person.

FIERI FACIAS - A writ of execution commanding the sheriff to levy and collect the amount of a judgment from the goods and chattels of the judgment debtor.

FINDING OF FACT - Determination from proof or judicial notice of the existence of a fact. A ruling implies a supporting finding of fact; no separate or formal finding is required unless required by a statute of this state.

FISCAL - Relating to accounts or the management of revenue.

FORECLOSURE (sale) - A sale of mortgaged property to obtain satisfaction of the mortgage out of the sale proceeds.

FORFEITURE - A penalty, a fine.

FORGERY - Fabricating or producing falsely, counterfeited.

FORTUITOUS - Accidental.

FORUM - A court of justice; a place of jurisdiction.

FRAUD - Deception; trickery.

FREEHOLDER - One who owns real property.

FUNGIBLE - Of such kind or nature that one specimen or part may be used in the place of another.

G

GARNISHEE - Person garnished.

GARNISHMENT - A legal process to reach the money or effects of a defendant, in the possession or control of a third person.

GRAND JURY - Not less than 16, not more than 23 citizens of a county sworn to inquire into crimes committed or triable in the county.

GRANT - To agree to; convey, especially real property.

GRANTEE - The person to whom a grant is made.

GRANTOR - The person by whom a grant is made.

GRATUITOUS - Given without a return, compensation or consideration.

GRAVAMEN - The grievance complained of or the substantial cause of a criminal action.

GUARANTY (n.) - A promise to answer for the payment of some debt, or the performance of some duty, in case of the failure of another person, who, in the first instance, is liable for such payment or performance.

GUARDIAN - The person, committee, or other representative authorized by law to protect the person or estate or both of an incompetent (or of a *sui juris* person having a guardian) and to act for him in matters affecting his person or property or both. An incompetent is a person under disability imposed by law.

GUILTY - Establishment of the fact that one has committed a breach of conduct; especially, a violation of law.

H

HABEAS CORPUS - You have the body; the name given to a variety of writs, having for their object to bring a party before a court or judge for decision as to whether such person is being lawfully held prisoner.

HABENDUM - In conveyancing; it is the clause in a deed conveying land which defines the extent of ownership to be held by the grantee.

HEARING - A proceeding whereby the arguments of the interested parties are heared.

HEARSAY - A type of testimony given by a witness who relates, not what he knows personally, but what others have told hi, or what he has heard said by others.

HEARSAY RULE, THE - (a) "Hearsay evidence" is evidence of a statement that was made other than by a witness while testifying at the hearing and that is offered to prove the truth of the matter stated; (b) Except as provided by law, hearsay evidence is inadmissible; (c) This section shall be known and may be cited as the hearsay rule.

HEIR - Generally, one who inherits property, real or personal.

HOLDER OF THE PRIVILEGE - (a) The client when he has no guardian or conservator; (b) A guardian or conservator of the client when the client has a guardian or conservator; (c) The personal representative of the client if the client is dead; (d) A successor, assign, trustee in dissolution, or any similar representative of a firm, association, organization, partnership, business trust, corporation, or public entity that is no longer in existence.

HUNG JURY - One so divided that they can't agree on a verdict.

HUSBAND-WIFE PRIVILEGE - An accused in a criminal proceeding has a privilege to prevent his spouse from testifying against him.

HYPOTHECATE - To pledge a thing without delivering it to the pledgee.

HYPOTHESIS - A supposition, assumption, or toehry.

I

I.E. (id est) - That is.

IB., OR IBID.(ibidem) - In the same place; used to refer to a legal reference previously cited to avoid repeating the entire citation.

ILLICIT - Prohibited; unlawful.

ILLUSORY - Deceiving by false appearance.

IMMUNITY - Exemption.

IMPEACH - To accuse, to dispute.

IMPEDIMENTS - Disabilities, or hindrances.

IMPLEAD - To sue or prosecute by due course of law.

IMPUTED - Attributed or charged to.

IN LOCO PARENTIS - In place of parent, a guardian.

IN TOTO - In the whole; completely.

INCHOATE - Imperfect; unfinished.

INCOMMUNICADO - Denial of the right of a prisoner to communicate with friends or relatives.

INCOMPETENT - One who is incapable of caring for his own affairs because he is mentally deficient or undeveloped.

INCRIMINATION - A matter will incriminate a person if it constitutes, or forms an essential part of, or, taken in connection with other matters disclosed, is a basis for a reasonable inference of such a violation of the laws of this State as to subject him to liability to punishment therefor, unless he has become for any reason permanently immune from punishment for such violation.

INCUMBRANCE - Generally a claim, lien, charge or liability attached to and binding real property.

INDEMNIFY - To secure against loss or damage; also, to make reimbursement to one for a loss already incurred by him.

INDEMNITY - An agreement to reimburse another person in case of an anticipated loss falling upon him.

INDICIA - Signs; indications.

INDICTMENT - An accusation in writing found and presented by a grand jury charging that a person has committed a crime.

INDORSE - To write a name on the back of a legal paper or document, generally, a negotiable instrument

INDUCEMENT - Cause or reason why a thing is done or that which incites the person to do the act or commit a crime; the motive for the criminal act.

INFANT - In civil cases one under 21 years of age.

INFORMATION - A formal accusation of crime made by a prosecuting attorney.

INFRA - Below, under; this word occurring by itself in a publication refers the reader to a future part of the publication.

INGRESS - The act of going into.

INJUNCTION - A writ or order by the court requiring a person, generally, to do or to refrain from doing an act.

INSOLVENT - The condition of a person who is unable to pay his debts.

INSTRUCTION - A direction given by the judge to the jury concerning the law of the case.

INTERIM - In the meantime; time intervening.

INTERLOCUTORY - Temporary, not final; something intervening between the commencement and the end of a suit which decides some point or matter, but is not a final decision of the whole controversy.

INTERROGATORIES - A series of formal written questions used in the examination of a party or a witness usually prior to a trial.

INTESTATE - A person who dies without a will.

INURE - To result, to take effect.

IPSO FACTO - By the fact iself; by the mere fact.

ISSUE (n.) The disputed point or question in a case,

J

JEOPARDY - Danger, hazard, peril.

JOINDER - Joining; uniting with another person in some legal steps or proceeding.

JOINT - United; combined.

JUDGE - Member or members or representative or representatives of a court conducting a trial or hearing at which evidence is introduced.

JUDGMENT - The official decision of a court of justice.

JUDICIAL OR JUDICIARY - Relating to or connected with the administration of justice.

JURAT - The clause written at the foot of an affidavit, stating when, where and before whom such affidavit was sworn.

JURISDICTION - The authority to hear and determine controversies between parties.

JURISPRUDENCE - The philosophy of law.

JURY - A body of persons legally selected to inquire into any matter of fact, and to render their verdict according to the evidence.

L

LACHES - The failure to diligently assert a right, which results in a refusal to allow relief.

LANDLORD AND TENANT - A phrase used to denote the legal relation existing between the owner and occupant of real estate.

LARCENY - Stealing personal property belonging to another.

LATENT - Hidden; that which does not appear on the face of a thing.

LAW - Includes constitutional, statutory, and decisional law.

LAWYER-CLIENT PRIVILEGE - (1) A "client" is a person, public officer, or corporation, association, or other organization or entity, either public or private, who is rendered professional legal services by a lawyer, or who consults a lawyer with a view to obtaining professional legal services from him; (2) A "lawyer" is a person authorized, or reasonably believed by the client to be authorized, to practice law in any state or nation; (3) A "representative of the lawyer" is one employed to assist the lawyer in the rendition of professional legal services; (4) A communication is "confidential" if not intended to be disclosed to third persons other than those to whom disclosure is in furtherance of the rendition of professional legal services to the client or those reasonably necessary for the transmission of the communication.

General rule of privilege - A client has a privilege to refuse to disclose and to prevent any other person from disclosing confidential communications made for the purpose of facilitating the rendition of professional legal services to the client, (1) between himself or his representative and his lawyer or his lawyer's representative, or (2) between his lawyer and the lawyer's representative, or (3) by him or his lawyer to a lawyer representing another in a matter of common interest, or (4) between representatives of the client or between the client and a representative of the client, or (5) between lawyers representing the client.

LEADING QUESTION - Question that suggests to the witness the answer that the examining party desires.

LEASE - A contract by which one conveys real estate for a limited time usually for a specified rent; personal property also may be leased.

LEGISLATION - The act of enacting laws.

LEGITIMATE - Lawful.

LESSEE - One to whom a lease is given.

LESSOR - One who grants a lease

LEVY - A collecting or exacting by authority.

LIABLE - Responsible; bound or obligated in law or equity.

LIBEL (v.) - To defame or injure a person's reputation by a published writing.

(n.) - The initial pleading on the part of the plaintiff in an admiralty proceeding.

LIEN - A hold or claim which one person has upon the property of another as a security for some debt or charge.

LIQUIDATED - Fixed; settled.

LIS PENDENS - A pending civil or criminal action.

LITERAL - According to the language.

LITIGANT - A party to a lawsuit.

LITATION - A judicial controversy.

LOCUS - A place.

LOCUS DELICTI - Place of the crime.

LOCUS POENITENTIAE - The abandoning or giving up of one's intention to commit some crime before it is fully completed or abandoning a conspiracy before its purpose is accomplished.

M

MALFEASANCE - To do a wrongful act.

MALICE - The doing of a wrongful act Intentionally without just cause or excuse.

MANDAMUS - The name of a writ issued by a court to enforce the performance of some public duty.

MANDATORY (adj.) Containing a command.

MARITIME - Pertaining to the sea or to commerce thereon.

MARSHALING - Arranging or disposing of in order.

MAXIM - An established principle or proposition.

MINISTERIAL - That which involves obedience to instruction, but demands no special discretion, judgment or skill.

MISAPPROPRIATE - Dealing fraudulently with property entrusted to one.

MISDEMEANOR - A crime less than a felony and punishable by a fine or imprisonment for less than one year.

MISFEASANCE - Improper performance of a lawful act.

MISREPRESENTATION - An untrue representation of facts.

MITIGATE - To make or become less severe, harsh.

MITTIMUS - A warrant of commitment to prison.

MOOT (adj.) Unsettled, undecided, not necessary to be decided.

MORTGAGE - A conveyance of property upon condition, as security for the payment of a debt or the performance of a duty, and to become void upon payment or performance according to the stipulated terms.

MORTGAGEE - A person to whom property is mortgaged.

MORTGAGOR - One who gives a mortgage.

MOTION - In legal proceedings, a "motion" is an application, either written or oral, addressed to the court by a party to an action or a suit requesting the ruling of the court on a matter of law.

MUTUALITY - Reciprocation.

N

NEGLIGENCE - The failure to exercise that degree of care which an ordinarily prudent person would exercise under like circumstances.

NEGOTIABLE (instrument) - Any instrument obligating the payment of money which is transferable from one person to another by endorsement and delivery or by delivery only.

NEGOTIATE - To transact business; to transfer a negotiable instrument; to seek agreement for the amicable disposition of a controversy or case.

NOLLE PROSEQUI - A formal entry upon the record, by the plaintiff in a civil suit or the prosecuting officer in a criminal action, by which he declares that he "will no further prosecute" the case.

NOLO CONTENDERE - The name of a plea in a criminal action, having the same effect as a plea of guilty; but not constituting a direct admission of guilt.

NOMINAL - Not real or substantial.

NOMINAL DAMAGES - Award of a trifling sum where no substantial injury is proved to have been sustained.

NONFEASANCE - Neglect of duty.

NOVATION - The substitution of a new debt or obligation for an existing one.

NUNC PRO TUNC - A phrase applied to acts allowed to be done after the time when they should be done, with a retroactive effect.("Now for then.")

O

OATH - Oath includes affirmation or declaration under penalty of perjury.

OBITER DICTUM - Opinion expressed by a court on a matter not essentially involved in a case and hence not a decision; also called dicta, if plural.

OBJECT (v.) - To oppose as improper or illegal and referring the question of its propriety or legality to the court.

OBLIGATION - A legal duty, by which a person is bound to do or not to do a certain thing.

OBLIGEE - The person to whom an obligation is owed.

OBLIGOR - The person who is to perform the obligation.

OFFER (v.) - To present for acceptance or rejection.

(n.) - A proposal to do a thing, usually a proposal to make a contract.

OFFICIAL INFORMATION - Information within the custody or control of a department or agency of the government the disclosure of which is shown to be contrary to the public interest.

OFFSET - A deduction.

ONUS PROBANDI - Burden of proof.

OPINION - The statement by a judge of the decision reached in a case, giving the law as applied to the case and giving reasons for the judgment; also a belief or view.

OPTION - The exercise of the power of choice; also a privilege existing in one person, for which he has paid money, which gives him the right to buy or sell real or personal property at a given price within a specified time.

ORDER - A rule or regulation; every direction of a court or judge made or entered in writing but not including a judgment.

ORDINANCE - Generally, a rule established by authority; also commonly used to designate the legislative acts of a municipal corporation.

ORIGINAL - Writing or recording itself or any counterpart intended to have the same effect by a person executing or issuing it. An "original" of a photograph includes the negative or any print therefrom. If data are stored in a computer or similar device, any printout or other output readable by sight, shown to reflect the data accurately, is an "original."

OVERT - Open, manifest.

P

PANEL - A group of jurors selected to serve during a term of the court.

PARENS PATRIAE - Sovereign power of a state to protect or be a guardian over children and incompetents.

PAROL - Oral or verbal.

PAROLE - To release one in prison before the expiration of his sentence, conditionally.

PARITY - Equality in purchasing power between the farmer and other segments of the economy.

PARTITION - A legal division of real or personal property between one or more owners.

PARTNERSHIP - An association of two or more persons to carry on as co-owners a business for profit.

PATENT (adj.) - Evident.

(n.) - A grant of some privilege, property, or authority, made by the government or sovereign of a country to one or more individuals.

PECULATION - Stealing.

PECUNIARY - Monetary.

PENULTIMATE - Next to the last.

PER CURIAM - A phrase used in the report of a decision to distinguish an opinion of the whole court from an opinion written by any one judge.

PER SE - In itself; taken alone.

PERCEIVE - To acquire knowledge through one's senses.

PEREMPTORY - Imperative; absolute.

PERJURY - To lie or state falsely under oath.

PERPETUITY - Perpetual existence; also the quality or condition of an estate limited so that it will not take effect or vest within the period fixed by law.

PERSON - Includes a natural person, firm, association, organization, partnership, business trust, corporation, or public entity.

PERSONAL PROPERTY - Includes money, goods, chattels, things in action, and evidences of debt.

PERSONALTY - Short term for personal property.

PETITION - An application in writing for an order of the court, stating the circumstances upon which it is founded and requesting any order or other relief from a court.

PLAINTIFF - A person who brings a court action.

PLEA - A pleading in a suit or action.

PLEADINGS - Formal allegations made by the parties of their respective claims and defenses, for the judgment of the court.

PLEDGE - A deposit of personal property as a security for the performance of an act.

PLEDGEE - The party to whom goods are delivered in pledge.

PLEDGOR - The party delivering goods in pledge.

PLENARY - Full; complete.

POLICE POWER - Inherent power of the state or its political subdivisions to enact laws within constitutional limits to promote the general welfare of society or the community.

POLLING THE JURY - Call the names of persons on a jury and requiring each juror to declare what his verdict is before it is legally recorded.

POST MORTEM - After death.

POWER OF ATTORNEY - A writing authorizing one to act for another.

PRECEPT - An order, warrant, or writ issued to an officer or body of officers, commanding him or them to do some act within the scope of his or their powers.

PRELIMINARY FACT - Fact upon the existence or nonexistence of which depends the admissibility or inadmissibility of evidence. The phrase "the admissibility or inadmissibility of evidence" includes the qualification or disqualification of a person to be a witness and the existence or nonexistence of a privilege.

PREPONDERANCE - Outweighing.

PRESENTMENT - A report by a grand jury on something they have investigated on their own knowledge.

PRESUMPTION - An assumption of fact resulting from a rule of law which requires such fact to be assumed from another fact or group of facts found or otherwise established in the action.

PRIMA FACUE - At first sight.

PRIMA FACIE CASE - A case where the evidence is very patent against the defendant.

PRINCIPAL - The source of authority or rights; a person primarily liable as differentiated from "principle" as a primary or basic doctrine.

PRO AND CON - For and against.

PRO RATA - Proportionally.

PROBATE - Relating to proof, especially to the proof of wills.

PROBATIVE - Tending to prove.

PROCEDURE - In law, this term generally denotes rules which are established by the Federal, State, or local Governments regarding the types of pleading and courtroom practice which must be followed by the parties involved in a criminal or civil case.

PROCLAMATION - A public notice by an official of some order, intended action, or state of facts.

PROFFERED EVIDENCE - The admissibility or inadmissibility of which is dependent upon the existence or nonexistence of a preliminary fact.

PROMISSORY (NOTE) - A promise in writing to pay a specified sum at an expressed time, or on demand, or at sight, to a named person, or to his order, or bearer.

PROOF - The establishment by evidence of a requisite degree of belief concerning a fact in the mind of the trier of fact or the court.

PROPERTY - Includes both real and personal property.

PROPRIETARY (adj.) - Relating or pertaining to ownership; usually a single owner.

PROSECUTE - To carry on an action or other judicial proceeding; to proceed against a person criminally.

PROVISO - A limitation or condition in a legal instrument.

PROXIMATE - Immediate; nearest

PUBLIC EMPLOYEE - An officer, agent, or employee of a public entity.

PUBLIC ENTITY - Includes a national, state, county, city and county, city, district, public authority, public agency, or any other political subdivision or public corporation, whether foreign or domestic.

PUBLIC OFFICIAL - Includes an official of a political dubdivision of such state or territory and of a municipality.

PUNITIVE - Relating to punishment.

Q

QUASH - To make void.

QUASI - As if; as it were.

QUID PRO QUO - Something for something; the giving of one valuable thing for another.

QUITCLAIM (v.) - To release or relinquish claim or title to, especially in deeds to realty.

QUO WARRANTO - A legal procedure to test an official's right to a public office or the right to hold a franchise, or to hold an office in a domestic corporation.

R

RATIFY - To approve and sanction.

REAL PROPERTY - Includes lands, tenements, and hereditaments.

REALTY - A brief term for real property.

REBUT - To contradict; to refute, especially by evidence and arguments.

RECEIVER - A person who is appointed by the court to receive, and hold in trust property in litigation.

RECIDIVIST - Habitual criminal.

RECIPROCAL - Mutual.

RECOUPMENT - To keep back or get something which is due; also, it is the right of a defendant to have a deduction from the amount of the plaintiff's damages because the plaintiff has not fulfilled his part of the same contract.

RECROSS EXAMINATION - Examination of a witness by a cross-examiner subsequent to a redirect examination of the witness.

REDEEM - To release an estate or article from mortgage or pledge by paying the debt for which it stood as security.

REDIRECT EXAMINATION - Examination of a witness by the direct examiner subsequent to the cross-examination of the witness.

REFEREE - A person to whom a cause pending in a court is referred by the court, to take testimony, hear the parties, and report thereon to the court.

REFERENDUM - A method of submitting an important legislative or administrative matter to a direct vote of the people.

RELEVANT EVIDENCE - Evidence including evidence relevant to the credulity of a witness or hearsay declarant, having any tendency in reason to prove or disprove any disputed fact that is of consequence to the determination of the action.

REMAND - To send a case back to the lower court from which it came, for further proceedings.

REPLEVIN - An action to recover goods or chattels wrongfully taken or detained.

REPLY (REPLICATION) - Generally, a reply is what the plaintiff or other person who has instituted proceedings says in answer to the defendant's case.

RE JUDICATA - A thing judicially acted upon or decided.

RES ADJUDICATA - Doctrine that an issue or dispute litigated and determined in a case between the opposing parties is deemed permanently decided between these parties.

RESCIND (RECISSION) - To avoid or cancel a contract.

RESPONDENT - A defendant in a proceeding in chancery or admiralty; also, the person who contends against the appeal in a case.

RESTITUTION - In equity, it is the restoration of both parties to their original condition (when practicable), upon the rescission of a contract for fraud or similar cause.

RETROACTIVE (RETROSPECTIVE) - Looking back; effective as of a prior time.

REVERSED - A term used by appellate courts to indicate that the decision of the lower court in the case before it has been set aside.

REVOKE - To recall or cancel.

RIPARIAN (RIGHTS) - The rights of a person owning land containing or bordering on a water course or other body of water, such as lakes and rivers.

S

SALE - A contract whereby the ownership of property is transferred from one person to another for a sum of money or for any consideration.

SANCTION - A penalty or punishment provided as a means of enforcing obedience to a law; also, an authorization.

SATISFACTION - The discharge of an obligation by paying a party what is due to him; or what is awarded to him by the judgment of a court or otherwise.

SCIENTER - Knowingly; also, it is used in pleading to denote the defendant's guilty knowledge.

SCINTILLA - A spark; also the least particle.

SECRET OF STATE - Governmental secret relating to the national defense or the international relations of the United States.

SECURITY - Indemnification; the term is applied to an obligation, such as a mortgage or deed of trust, given by a debtor to insure the payment or performance of his debt, by furnishing the creditor with a resource to be used in case of the debtor's failure to fulfill the principal obligation.

SENTENCE - The judgment formally pronounced by the court or judge upon the defendant after his conviction in a criminal prosecution.

SET-OFF - A claim or demand which one party in an action credits against the claim of the opposing party.

SHALL and MAY - "Shall" is mandatory and "may" is permissive.

SITUS - Location.

SOVEREIGN - A person, body or state in which independent and supreme authority is vested.

STARE DECISIS - To follow decided cases.

STATE - "State" means this State, unless applied to the different parts of the United States. In the latter case, it includes any state, district, commonwealth, territory or insular possession of the United States, including the District of Columbia.

STATEMENT - (a) Oral or written verbal expression or (b) nonverbal conduct of a person intended by him as a substitute for oral or written verbal expression.

STATUTE - An act of the legislature. Includes a treaty.

STATUTE OF LIMITATION - A statute limiting the time to bring an action after the right of action has arisen.

STAY - To hold in abeyance an order of a court.

STIPULATION - Any agreement made by opposing attorneys regulating any matter incidental to the proceedings or trial.

SUBORDINATION (AGREEMENT) - An agreement making one's rights inferior to or of a lower rank than another's.

SUBORNATION - The crime of procuring a person to lie or to make false statements to a court.

SUBPOENA - A writ or order directed to a person, and requiring his attendance at a particular time and place to testify as a witness.

SUBPOENA DUCES TECUM - A subpoena used, not only for the purpose of compelling witnesses to attend in court, but also requiring them to bring with them books or documents which may be in their possession, and which may tend to elucidate the subject matter of the trial.

SUBROGATION - The substituting of one for another as a creditor, the new creditor succeeding to the former's rights.

SUBSIDY - A government grant to assist a private enterprise deemed advantageous to the public.

SUI GENERIS - Of the same kind.

SUIT - Any civil proceeding by a person or persons against another or others in a court of justice by which the plaintiff pursues the remedies afforded him by law.

SUMMONS - A notice to a defendant that an action against him has been commenced and requiring him to appear in court and answer the complaint.

SUPRA - Above; this word occurring by itself in a book refers the reader to a previous part of the book.

SURETY - A person who binds himself for the payment of a sum of money, or for the performance of something else, for another.

SURPLUSAGE - Extraneous or unnecessary matter.

SURVIVORSHIP - A term used when a person becomes entitled to property by reason of his having survived another person who had an interest in the property.

SUSPEND SENTENCE - Hold back a sentence pending good behavior of prisoner.

SYLLABUS - A note prefixed to a report, especially a case, giving a brief statement of the court's ruling on different issues of the case.

T

TALESMAN - Person summoned to fill a panel of jurors.

TENANT - One who holds or possesses lands by any kind of right or title; also, one who has the temporary use and occupation of real property owned by another person (landlord), the duration and terms of his tenancy being usually fixed by an instrument called "a lease."

TENDER - An offer of money; an expression of willingness to perform a contract according to its terms.

TERM - When used with reference to a court, it signifies the period of time during which the court holds a session, usually of several weeks or months duration.

TESTAMENTARY - Pertaining to a will or the administration of a will.

TESTATOR (male)

TESTATRIX (female) - One who makes or has made a testament or will.

TESTIFY (TESTIMONY) - To give evidence under oath as a witness.

TO WIT - That is to say; namely.

TORT - Wrong; injury to the person.

TRANSITORY - Passing from place to place.

TRESPASS - Entry into another's ground, illegally.

TRIAL - The examination of a cause, civil or criminal, before a judge who has jurisdiction over it, according to the laws of the land.

TRIER OF FACT - Includes (a) the jury and (b) the court when the court is trying an issue of fact other than one relating to the admissibility of evidence.

TRUST - A right of property, real or personal, held by one party for the benefit of another.

TRUSTEE - One who lawfully holds property in custody for the benefit of another.

U

UNAVAILABLE AS A WITNESS - The declarant is (1) Exempted or precluded on the ground of privilege from testifying concerning the matter to which his statement is relevant; (2) Disqualified from testifying to the matter; (3) Dead or unable to attend or to testify at the hearing because of then existing physical or mental illness or infirmity; (4) Absent from the hearing and the court is unable to compel his attendance by its process; or (5) Absent from the hearing and the proponent of his statement has exercised reasonable diligence but has been unable to procure his attendance by the court's process.

ULTRA VIRES - Acts beyond the scope and power of a corporation, association, etc.

UNILATERAL - One-sided; obligation upon, or act of one party.

USURY - Unlawful interest on a loan.

V

VACATE - To set aside; to move out.

VARIANCE - A discrepancy or disagreement between two instruments or two aspects of the same case, which by law should be consistent.

VENDEE - A purchaser or buyer.

VENDOR - The person who transfers property by sale, particularly real estate; the term "seller" is used more commonly for one who sells personal property.

VENIREMEN - Persons ordered to appear to serve on a jury or composing a panel of jurors.

VENUE - The place at which an action is tried, generally based on locality or judicial district in which an injury occurred or a material fact happened.

VERDICT - The formal decision or finding of a jury.

VERIFY - To confirm or substantiate by oath.

VEST - To accrue to.

VOID - Having no legal force or binding effect.

VOIR DIRE - Preliminary examination of a witness or a juror to test competence, interest, prejudice, etc.

W

WAIVE - To give up a right.

WAIVER - The intentional or voluntary relinquishment of a known right.

WARRANT (WARRANTY) (v.) - To promise that a certain fact or state of facts, in relation to the subject matter, is, or shall be, as it is represented to be.

WARRANT (n.) - A writ issued by a judge, or other competent authority, addressed to a sheriff, or other officer, requiring him to arrest the person therein named, and bring him before the judge or court to answer or be examined regarding the offense with which he is charged.

WRIT - An order or process issued in the name of the sovereign or in the name of a court or judicial officer, commanding the performance or nonperformance of some act.

WRITING - Handwriting, typewriting, printing, photostating, photographing and every other means of recording upon any tangible thing any form of communication or representation, including letters, words, pictures, sounds, or symbols, or combinations thereof.

WRITINGS AND RECORDINGS - Consists of letters, words, or numbers, or their equivalent, set down by handwriting, typewriting, printing, photostating, photographing, magnetic impulse, mechanical or electronic recording, or other form of data compilation.

Y

YEA AND NAY - Yes and no.

YELLOW DOG CONTRACT - A contract by which employer requires employee to sign an instrument promising as condition that he will not join a union during its continuance, and will be discharged if he does join.

Z

ZONING - The division of a city by legislative regulation into districts and the prescription and application in each district of regulations having to do with structural and architectural designs of buildings and of regulations prescribing use to which buildings within designated districts may be put.